Theatrum Fungorium

Volume III
by
Stanton F. Fink

Ex putredine fit luxuria vita

Acknowledgments
and Dedication

To my father, in whose books I discovered my first monsters.

To Will Caligan, whose help and encouragement is one of the primary reasons for this book's existence.

To Mariano Silvera, who should have had his own artbooks

To Doctor David Morafka, who helped teach me to be more picky with my information.

To Thomas Hegna, whose assistance and support continue being of incalculable importance.

To Nikolas Draper-Ivey, he who wields the sword of Ragnarok, and who has been awarded the Decorations of Omega; he who stands tall to cleave open the Heavens.

To David Jaxon, my eventual partner in crime.

To my friends, who helped push me to make this.

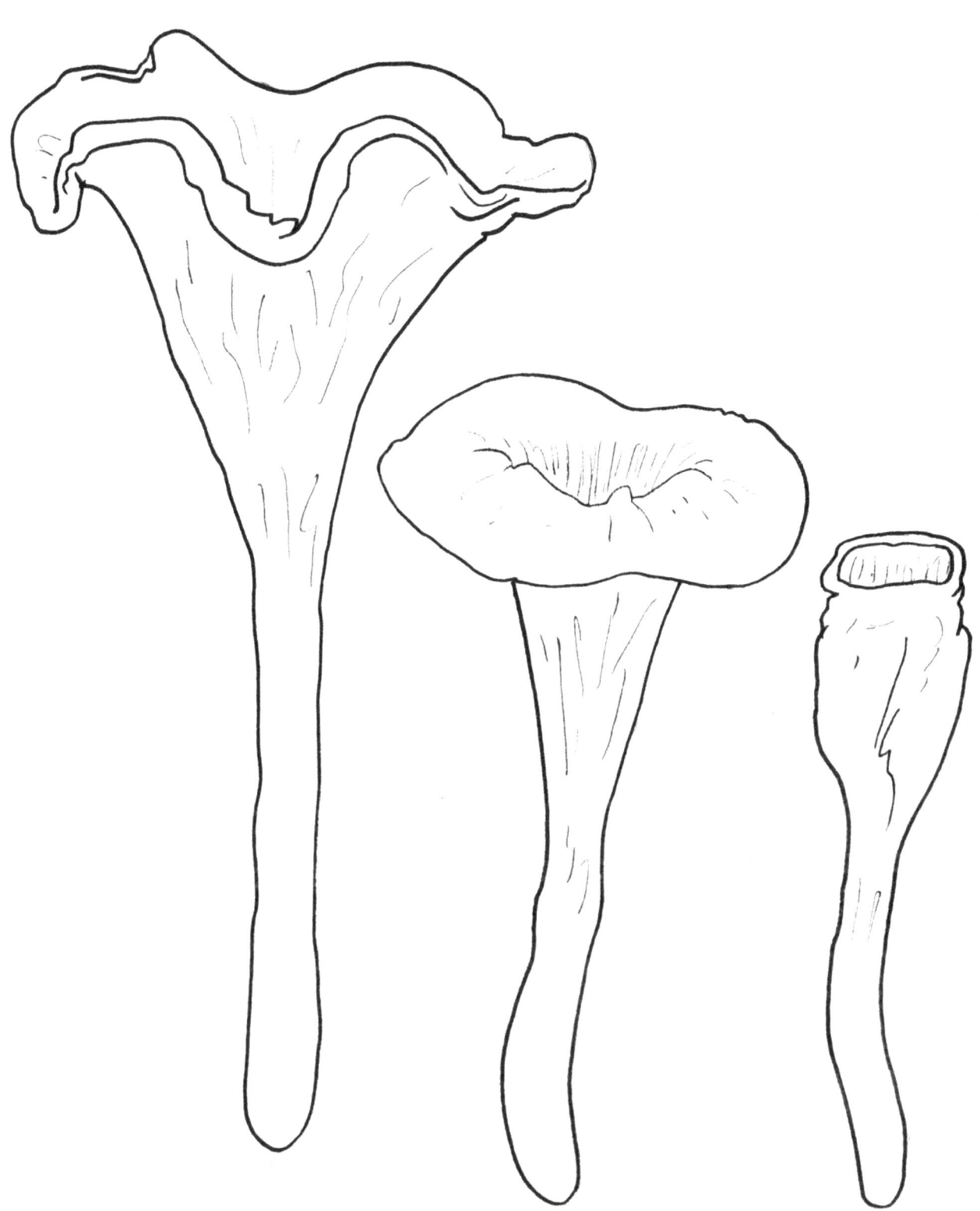

Table of Contents

Acknowledgments — page 2

Introduction — page 5

Glossary — page 6

   1. *Abrachium floriforme* — page 8

   2. *Austroboletus amazonicus* — page 10

   3. *Baorangia pseudocalopus* — page 12

   4. *Calostoma insigne* — page 14

   5. *Cantharellus congolensis* — page 16

   6. *Clathrus ruber* — page 18

   7. *Entoloma eugenei* — page 20

   8. *Imleria badia* — page 22

   9. *Lactarius deliciosus* — page 24

   10. *Lanmaoa asiatica* — page 26

   11. *Leotis viscosa* — page 28

   12. *Marasmius hudsonii* — page 30

   13. *Morchella esculenta* — page 32

   14. *Mycena epipterygia* — page 34

   15. *Mycena pura* — page 36

   16. *Podoserpula miranda* — page 38

   17. *Russula xerampelina* — page 40

   18. *Tricholoma equestre* — page 42

Bibliography — page 44

About the Artist — page 46

Introduction

This book is an artistic portfolio I've put together of various mushrooms and fungi I've drawn since 2023. I hope that my humble little coloring book will entice readers and colorers into learning more about fungi.

Having said this, please don't use my books as a mushroom field guide. I have limited ability in photorealism, and several species I've drawn are dangerous, if not deadly deadly poisonous.

Furthermore, I, the artist claim copyright of all art featured in this book, though I officially grant permission for personal or non-commercial use copies to be made. Other inquiries can be made to me via either apokryltaros@gmail.com or stanton.fink@protonmail.com

Glossary

- **Aquatic**- Living in water.
- **Egg**- A globular structure composed of a sac, and the developing or embryonic fruiting body contained within.
- **Fruiting Body**- The spore-bearing structure of a fungus, i.e., "mushroom."
- **Gleba**- The spongy, fleshy inner mass of spore-producing tissue found in some fungi, like earthstars or the tips of stinkhorn.
- **Haustorium**- The haustorium (plural "haustoria") is a modified hypha used by parasitic and other symbiotic fungi to penetrate the tissues of other organisms. In parasitic species, this is to take nutrients out of the host's tissue, while in mutualistic species, this is to facilitate nutrient exchange (often to consume sugar in exchange for minerals and nitrogen).
- **Hymenium**- The spore-bearing surface of a mushroom or fruiting body, it is found on the cap, or pileus, often its underside. Mushroom gills or bolete pores are derived from the hymenium (plural "hymenia")
- **Hypha**-The thread-like component of fungal tissue. Plural is "hyphae." Hyphae grow at their tips, and they are the basic unit of the root-like body of a fungus, termed a "mycellium."
- **Lamella**- The sheet-like, spore-producing organ that is the primary unit of mushroom gills. Plural is "lamellae." Lamellae are attached to the spore-bearing surface of the pileus, or hymenium.
- **Mushroom**- Officially, the term "mushroom" refers to the macroscopic, spore-bearing fruiting body of a fungus seasonally produced by the mycellium. A mushroom, in this sense, usually has a stem or stipe, a cap or pileus, a spore-bearing surface or hymenium, and gills or lamellae, or gleba. However, not all "mushrooms" will have all of these features (like puffballs and boletes). Colloquially, "mushroom" is often used to refer to both the fruiting bodies and mycellium, that is, the entire organism (such as the denizens of a mushroom growing kit).
- **Mycellium**- The mycellium (plural "mycellia") is a root-like mass of hyphae that serves as the main body of a fungus. Mycellia grow within or on top of their food sources (which also serve as their environment).
- **Mycorrhizal**- A mycorrhizal fungus forms a symbiotic relationship with plants through their hosts' root system. Ectomycorrhizal fungi form a sheath around plants' rootlets.
- **Pileus**- The cap of a mushroom. The pileus houses the hymenium.
- **Spore**- The primary reproductive unit of a fungus; spores can be produced both sexually (from the fusion of haploid tissues), or asexually. Fungal reproduction is very complicated, and far, far, far beyond my own personal understanding, let alone ability to explain in small (or even big) words.
- **Stipe**- The stalk or stem of a mushroom or other fungal fruiting body.
- **Terrestrial**- Living on land.

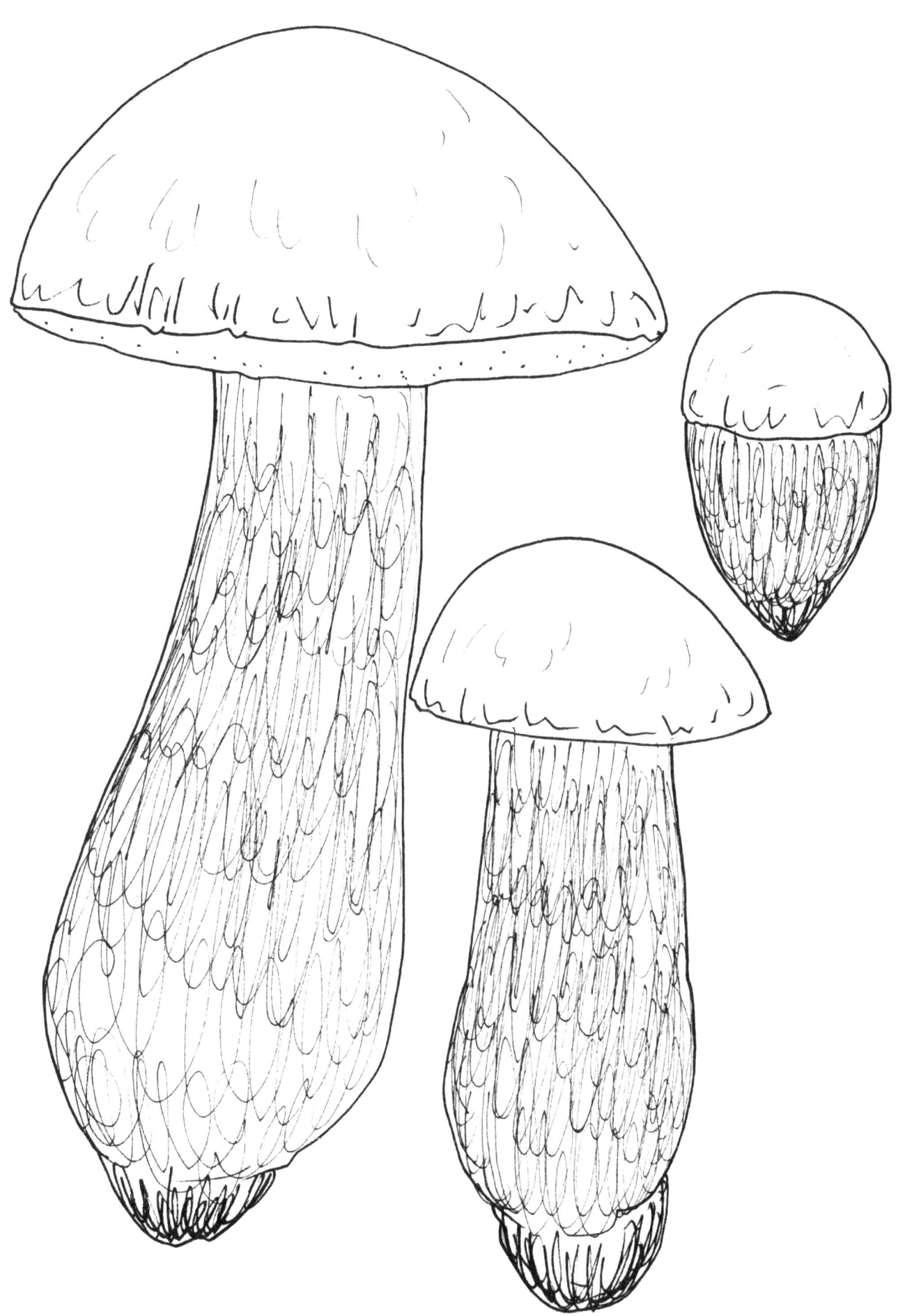

Name *Abrachium floriforme*

Location Atlantic coastal rainforests of Brazil.

Comments *Abrachium floriforme*, synonym "*Aseroë floriformis*," is a rare species of stinkhorn found in the Atlantic coastal rainforests of Northeastern Brazil. It is closely related to the anemone stinkhorns of *Aseroe*, though, differs by how the fruiting body terminates in a disc, and not branches.

The egg is whitish or yellow, and is 1 to 2 centimeters wide. The raspberry pink to raspberry red stipe grows 3 to 4 centimeter tall, and the tip opens into a yellow to pink, sunflower-like disc 1.5 to 3.5 centimeters in diameter. The olive-brown gleba, or spore-fluid sits in a puddle in the center of the disc, and smells of fresh cattle manure when fresh. Flies and other coprophilic insects are attracted to the fungus, eat the spore-laden gleba, and then deposit the digested spores on rotten wood which the fungus feeds on.

Destruction of the Brazilian rainforests is the primary threat to this stinkhorn, which is labeled as "vulnerable" by conservation groups.

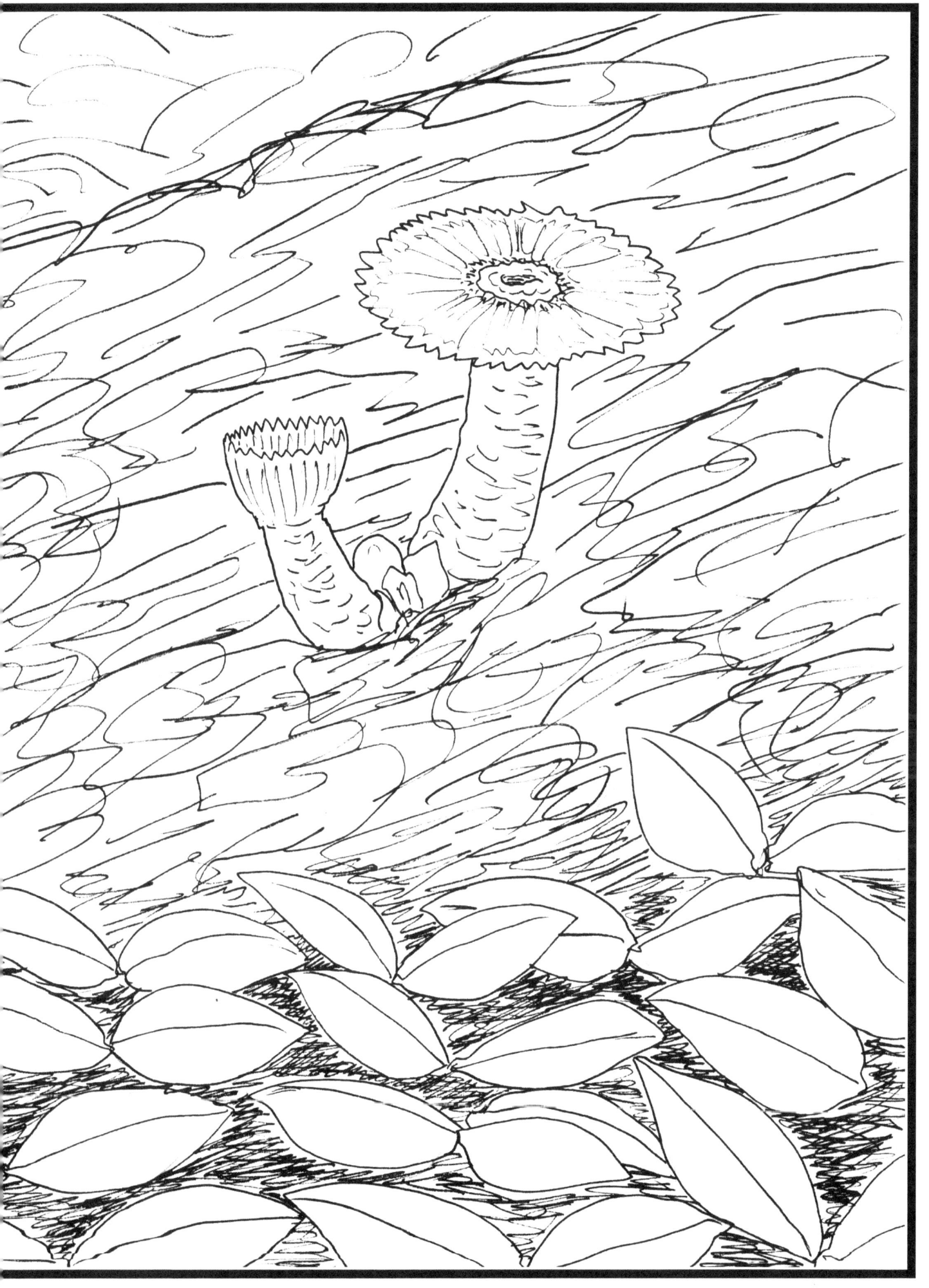

Name *Austroboletus amazonicus*

Location Amazon rainforests in Southeastern Columbia.

Comments *Austroboletus amazonicus* is a critically endangered species of bolete that is an endomycorrhizal symbiote of the endangered species of dipterocarp tree, *Pseudomonotes tropenbosii*, which is restricted to eight small populations in the Columbian Amazon rainforest in Southeastern Columbia. The fruiting body is small, covered in whitish tufts, similar to the tufts of the related pineapple bolete, *Boletellus ananas,* or the warts of the unrelated fly agaric, *Amanita muscaria.* When the tufts erode away, the mushroom becomes a pale tan. The pores on the underside of the pileus are large, forming a honeycomb pattern on the hymenium.

So far, *A. amazonicus* has only been collected from three of the 8 sites in the Columbian Amazon where its host, *P. tropenbosii*, grows. Because there are indigenous villages nearby, the mushroom's greatest threat, in addition to general deforestation, is habitat disturbance for agriculture.

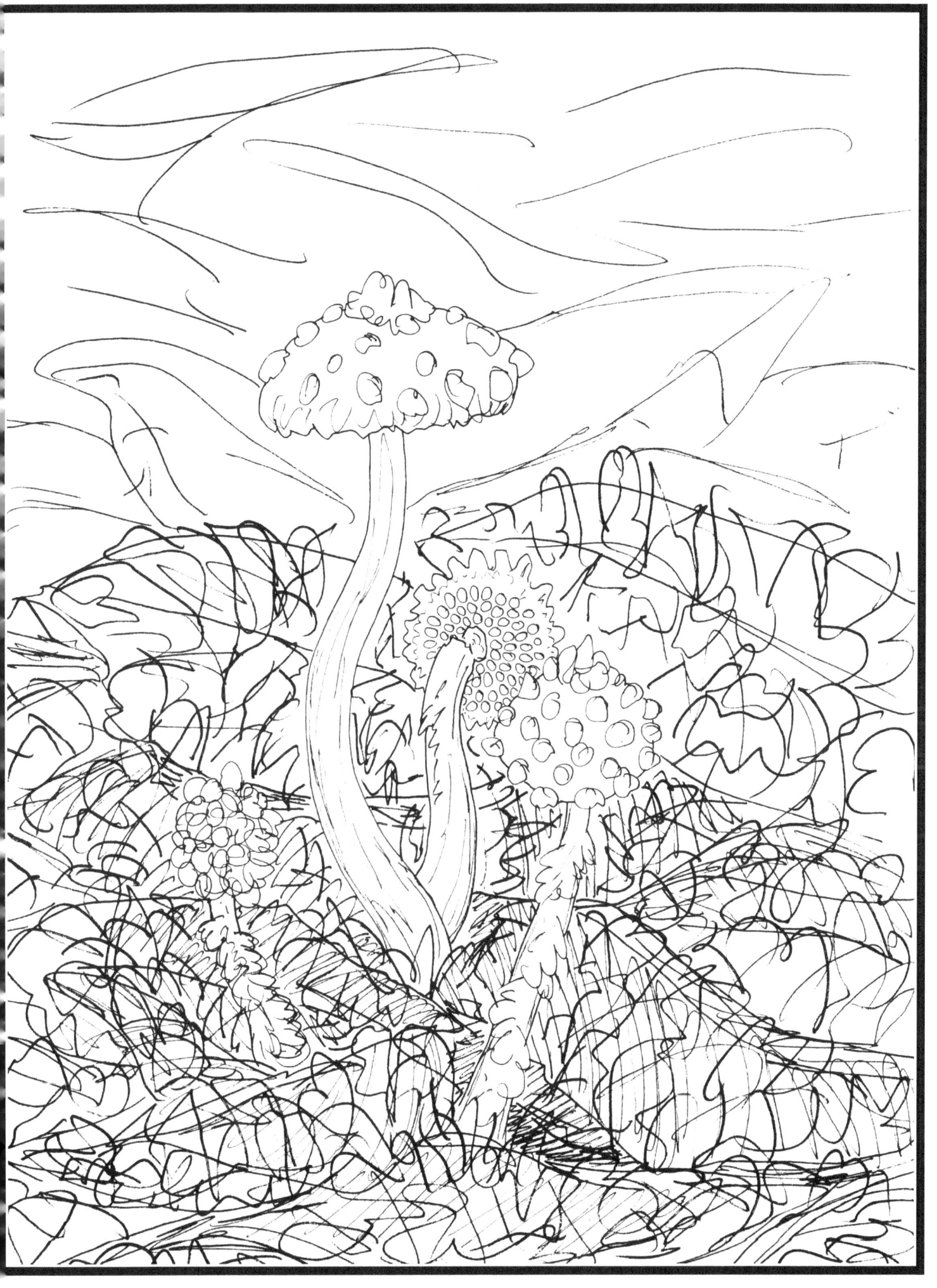

Name *Baorangia pseudocalopus*

Location Originally hardwood and conifer forests of Europe, the Mediterranean Basin, and the Middle East, now everywhere.

Comments The Chinese or False Bitter Bolete, *Baorangia pseudocalopus*, synonym "*Boletus pseudocalopus*," is a species of bolete found in mixed warm temperate to subtropical forests of Japan, the Korean Peninsula, and Hubei, Sichuan and Yunnan Provinces, China. *B. pseudocalopus* is an ectomycorrhizal symbiote of *Pinus* pine trees and fagacid trees (i.e., beeches, walnuts and their relatives).

The fruiting body resembles those of the bitter boletus, *Tylopilus felleus*, with a grayish rose to grayish red or red-brown, 5 to 15 centimeter diameter pileus and a yellow stipe flushed red, 5 centimeters tall. The pileus is flatter, and the stipe thinner in *B. pseudocalopus*.

Similar to *T. felleus*, the Chinese bitter bolete has a terrible, bitter taste, and causes gastrointestinal distress.

The generic name is derived from 薄瓢, meaning "thin hymenium/flesh," refering to how *B. pseudocalopus* and other boletes placed in the genus have the hymenium form a comparatively thin layer of tissue (usually up to 1 centimeter in thickness).

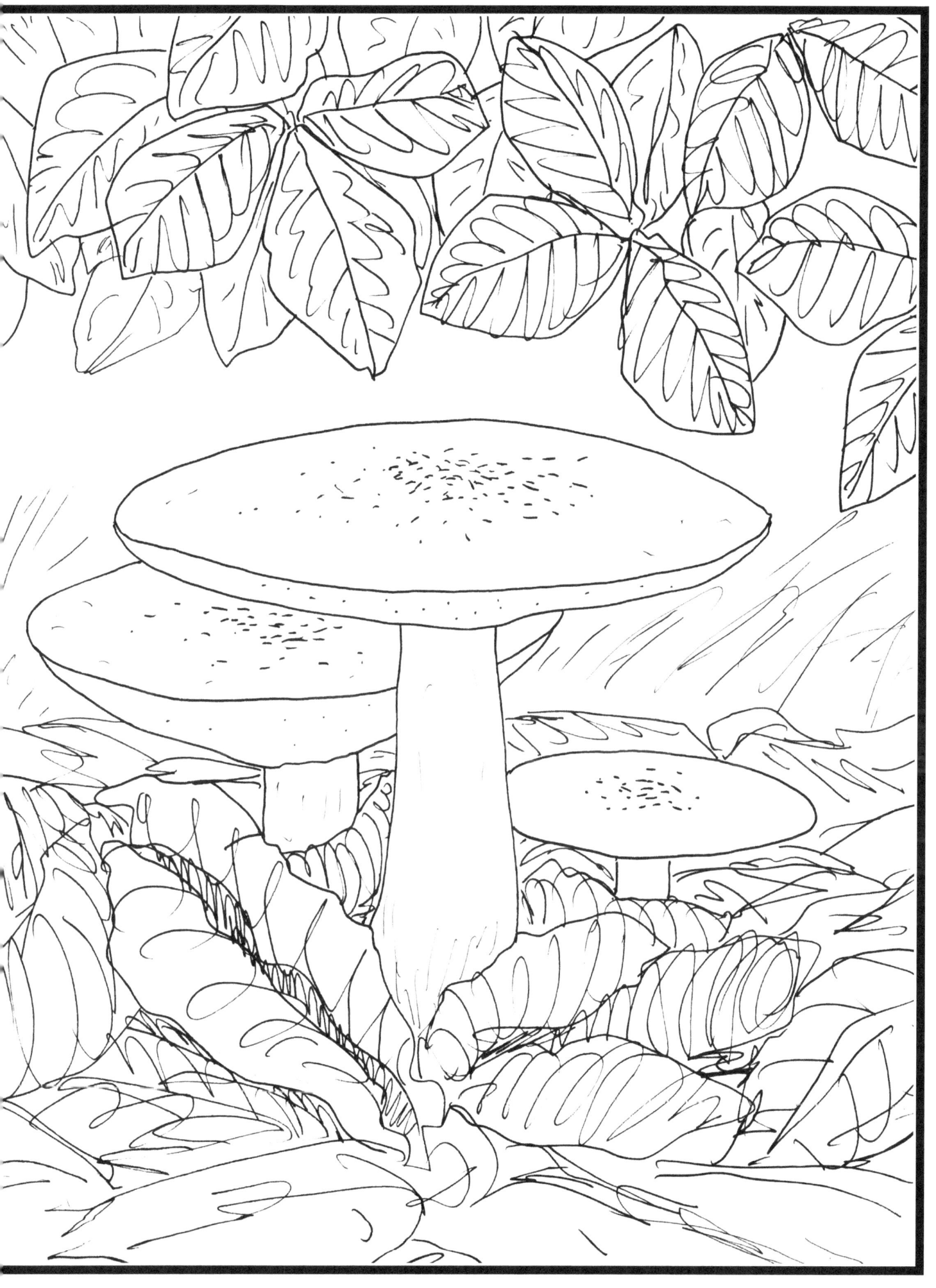

Name *Calostoma insigne*

Location Various tropical rainforests of Southeast Asia, Indonesia, Papau New Guinea, and Queensland, Australia.

Comments *Calostoma insigne*, called "เห็ดตาโต" (hedtato, or "big eye mushroom") in Thailand, is an endangered species of prettymouth, or puffball-in-aspic found as an ectomycorrhizal symbiote of various dipterocarp trees in rainforests from Southeast Asia to Queensland, Australia. Because of this specific association, together with the systemic destruction of Asian and Australian rainforests, *C. insigne* has a fragmented distribution limited to various dipterocarp stands spread across those regions of the world. The off-white to pure white fruiting body is large: with the gelatinous coating, or exoperidium, it can be 3 to 6 centimeters in diameter. Once the exoperidium peels away, the eyeball-like fruiting body is 2 to 3 centimeters in diameter, and rests atop a stipe that looks like a neat stalk of tentacles. The fruiting bodies appear during or upon the conclusion of the rainy season. *C. insigne* is easily confused with *C. japonica*, whose revealed fruiting body is more mayonnaise-colored, with a coral-colored "mouth."

The primary threat to *C. insigne* is the destruction of its host trees through deforestation, often for the creation of oil palm plantations and slash and burn agriculture. Some local peoples, primarily in Northern Thailand and Borneo, harvest *C. insigne* as food, either lightly steamed and added to sweet or spicy sauces as either a dessert or spicy condiment, or eaten raw as a prophylactic antidote for food poisoning and medicinal herb for promoting gut health. Some studies suggest it may have mild, anticancer properties.

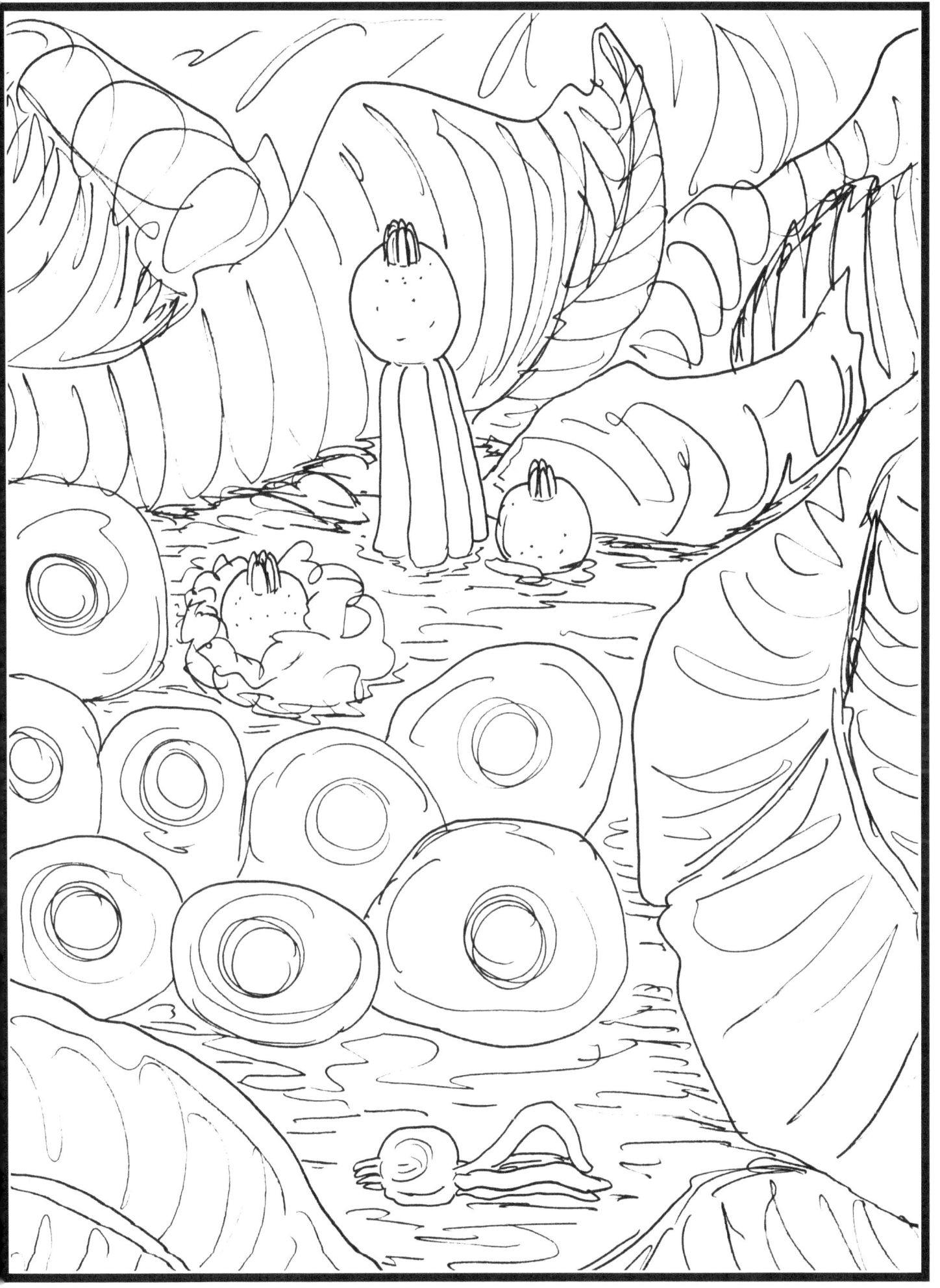

Name *Cantharellus congolensis*

Location Rainforests and tropical woodlands of Subsaharan Africa and Madagascar.

Comments *Cantharellus congolenesis* is a large chanterelle found throughout rainforests and tropical woodlands of Subsaharan Africa and Madagascar.

As with *C. cibarius*, *C. congolensis* has a pleasant, fruity odor that quickly dissipates upon being picked. Unlike most other chanterelles, the fruiting body of *C. congolensis* is a drab, speckled, brownish gray to "rotten leaf brown." The cap is 4 to 7 centimeters in diameter, and the stipe is 5 to 7 centimeters long. The mushroom is an ectomycorrhizal symbiote of Fabaceaen trees (trees in the bean family), preferring species of the genus *Julbernardia*, and various African species in the subfamily Caesalpinioideae.

C. congolensis is commonly gathered by local peoples, and are often seen in the company of chanterelles of *Afrocantharellus*. Despite being edible, many people shun it in favor of more colorful relatives under the mistaken assumption that *C. congolensis*' drab coloration means that it is allegedly poisonous.

Because of the wide range of *C. congolensis*, mycologists suspect it is actually a species complex of identical-looking species who are genetically distinct. However, this will take time and additional study to confirm.

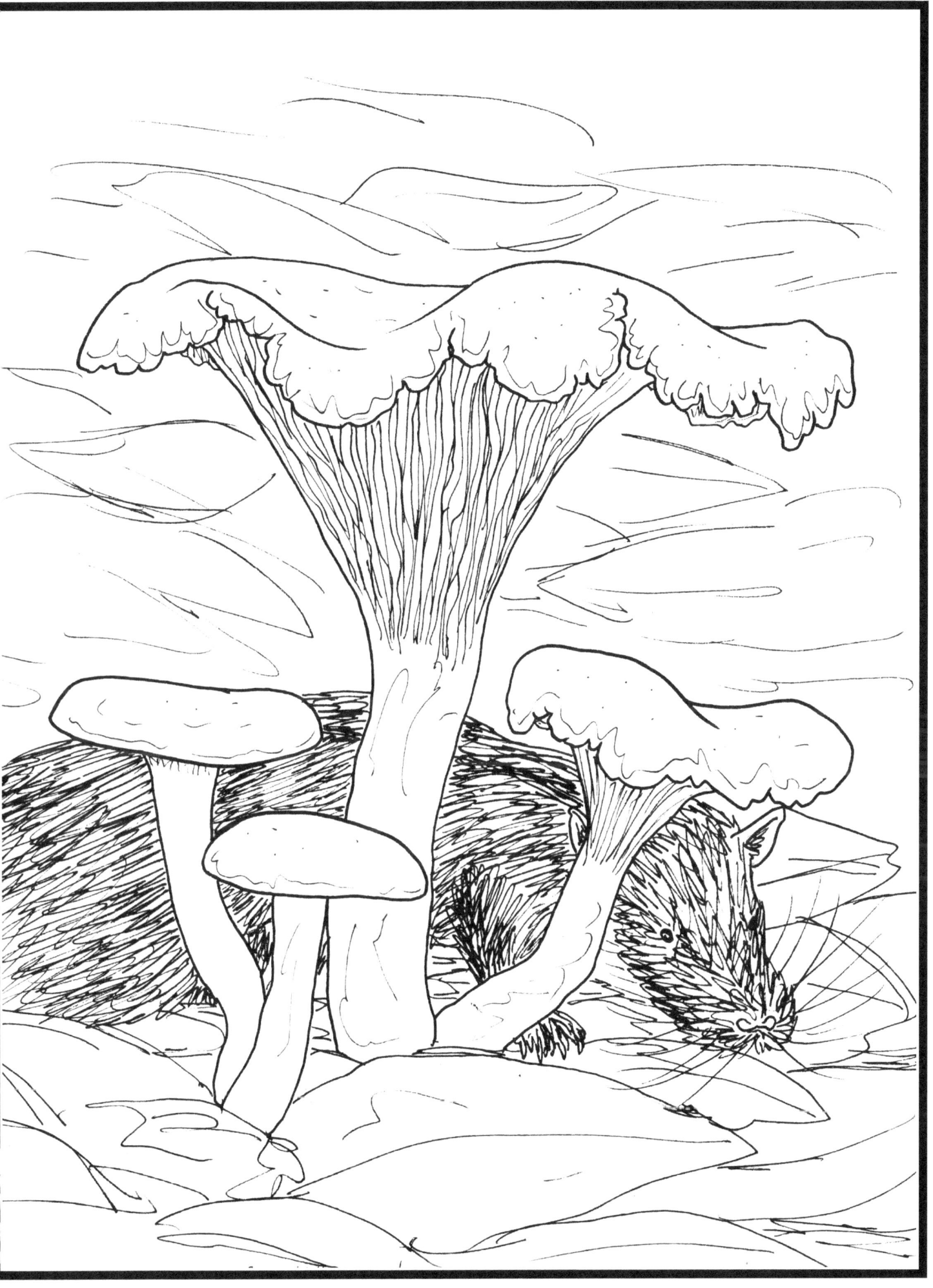

Name *Clathrus ruber*

Location Native to Southern to Central Europe, and Macaronesia (the Azores and Canary Islands). Introduced to the British Isles, North America, China, Austronesia, and Argentina.

Comments *Clathrus ruber*, the Lattice Stinkhorn, Basket Stinkhorn, Red Cage Fungus, or Witch's Heart, is a species of stinkhorn fungus, or "cage stinkhorn," with a large fruiting body in the form of a spherical, open-latticed cage or wiffle ball.

The pinkish to red fruiting body is large, growing up to 20 centimeters in diameter when fully mature. It hatches from a large egg about 6 centimeters in diameter, which is covered in a latticed membrane that, hilariously, looks like a tiny soccer ball. The gleba, or liquid spore mass is held and spread on the inside of the fruiting body: the gleba is initially a globe inside of the emerging fruiting body. The fruiting body collapses within 24 hours of hatching. The rotting meat odor of *C. ruber* is, allegedly, the vilest smelling of the entire stinkhorn family: there have been literal centuries of documentation of trained mycologists taking extremely egregious offense to the powerful stench (one mycologist threw her specimen out of a window when she could not tolerate waiting for it to dry). Unsurprisingly, the odor attracts all manner of carrion-feeding insects from houseflies to scarab beetles.

C. ruber is a saprophyte that feeds on rotting plant matter. It was originally native to open woodlands and meadows of Southern to Central Europe and Macaronesia, and has spread to other parts of the world due to the importation of infected wood mulch.

The miasmatic parfum of the fruiting body discourages most humans from eating *C. ruber* on principle. Additionally, there are many anecdotes of people succumbing to violent nausea and going into convulsions, seizures and comas due to consuming it.

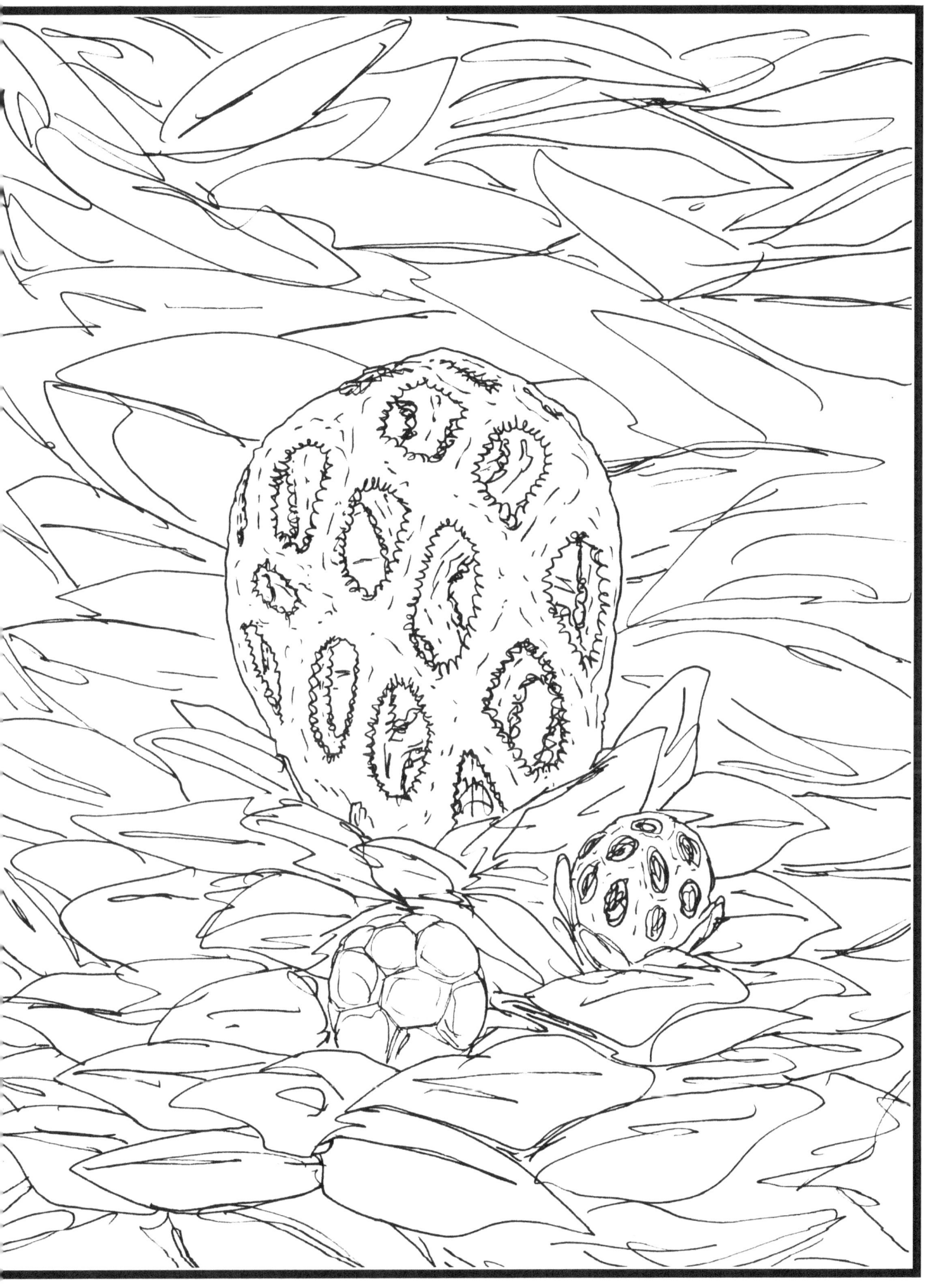

Name *Entoloma eugenei*

Location Hardwood forests of Eastern Siberia, Japan, Korea, and possibly Taiwan.

Comments *Entoloma eugenei* is a rare, indigo to azure blue mushroom first found in hardwood forests of the Russian Far East, and later in Japan and Korea. Specimens found in Taiwan attributed to *E. eugenei* may or may not be a different species, as the coloration of those tend to be indigo to purple-indigo.

The blue fruiting bodies grow up to 8 centimeters tall, and have caps up to 6 centimeters wide. Its edibility is unknown, but, even if it were edible, eating it would be prohibited as its rarity, coupled with threats imposed by logging-induced habitat loss has lead the International Union for the Conservation of Nature (IUCN) to put the species on the IUCN Red List as being endangered.

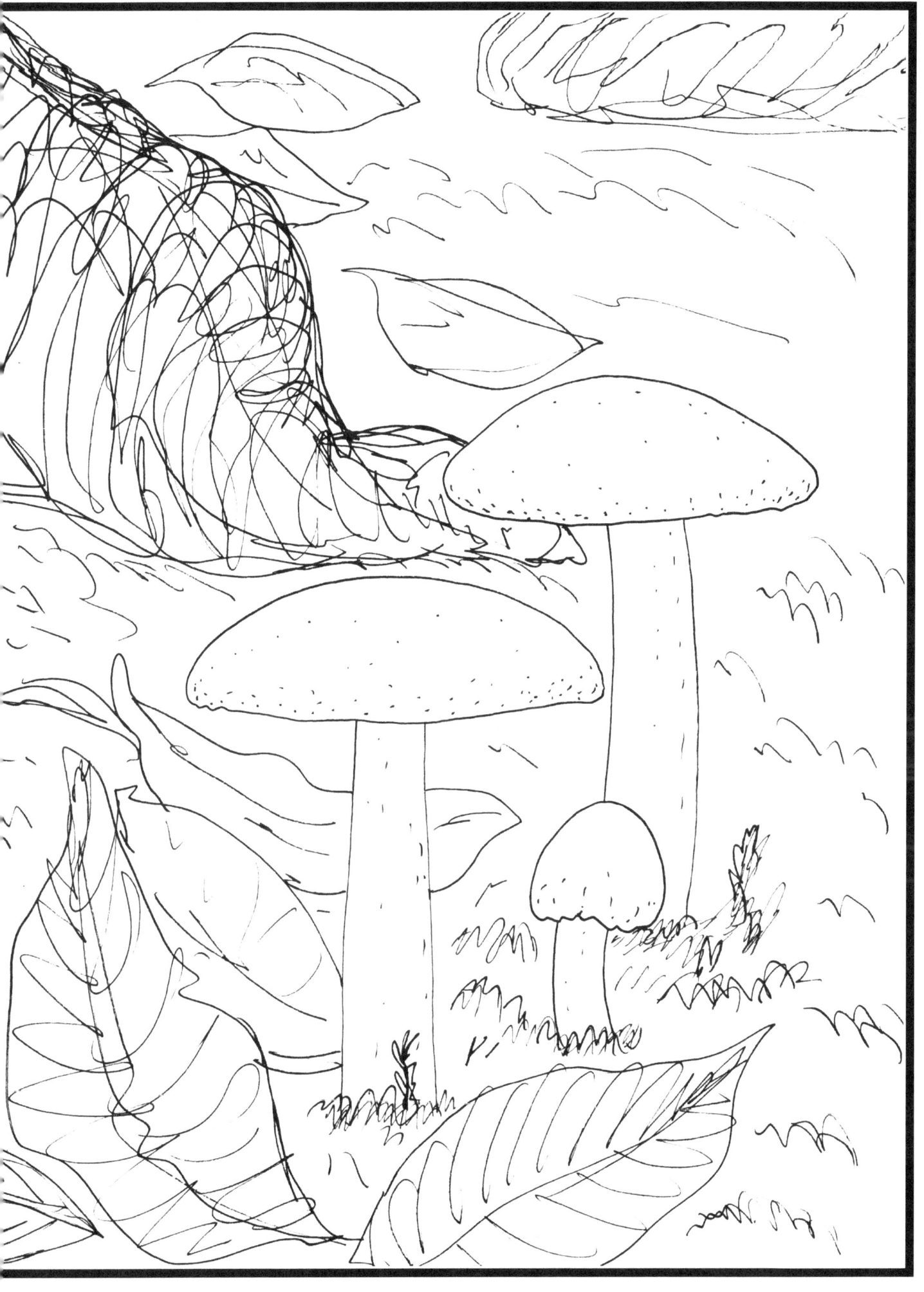

Name *Imleria badia*

Location Coniferous to mixed woodlands of Eurasia and North America.

Comments The Bay Bolete, or more offensively, the False Cep, currently *Imleria badia*, is an iconic bolete that lives as a saprophytic ectomycorrhizal symbiote of various conifers and fagacid trees.

The mature fruiting body is a shiny dark brown (chestnut-colored, or "bay horse brown"), with a pale beige or pale yellow pore surface that bruises bluish when injured. The fruiting body can grow up to 15 centimeters high, with a large cap up to 15 centimeters in diameter: the mature mushroom looks like a pretzel bun impaled on top of a breadstick.

The bay bolete can be safely eaten raw, but many mushroom connoisseurs denounce it as an inferior substitute for the porcini, *Boletus edulis*, due to the bay's lighter flavor. Thus the epithet of "false cep." Even so, the bay bolete is still regarded by less judgmental foragers as a delightful choice fungus. Bay boletes can bioaccumulate cadium from the environment, so those growing in places with high cadiums should be avoided, however.

The bay bolete was originally described as a subspecies of the chestnut bolete, then *Boletus castaneus* (now *Gyropilus castaneus*). After being promoted to full species, *"Boletus" badius* was then moved to the genus *Xerocomus*. When *Xerocomus* was determined to be polyphyletic, and *"Xerocomus" badius* was determined to be not closely related to other species of *Xerocomus*, it was moved to a new genus, *Imleria*, as *Imleria badia*, in 2014, in honor of the prodigious Belgian mycologist, Louis Imler.

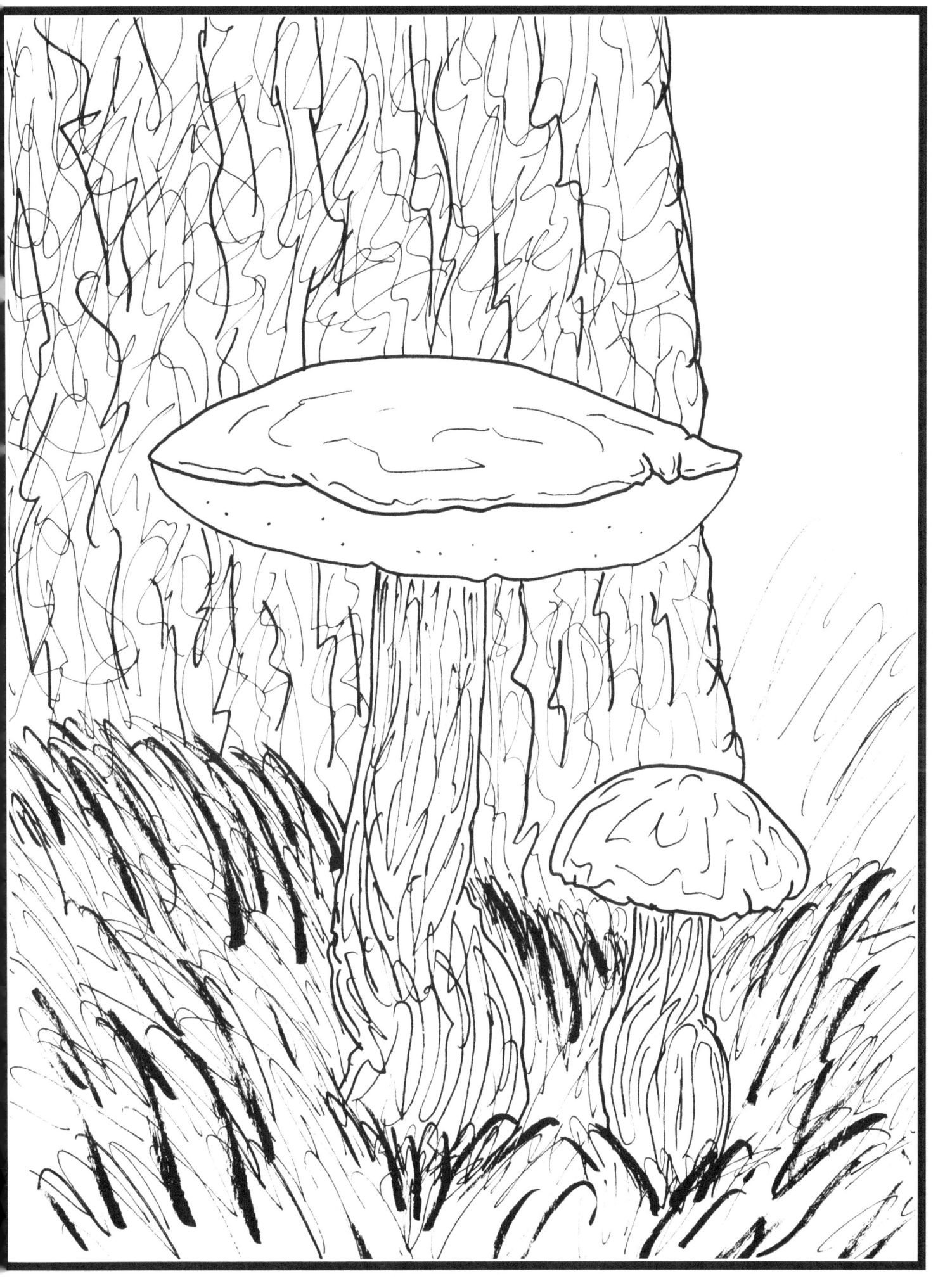

Name   *Lactarius deliciosus*

Location   Native to pine forests with acidic soils along the European Mediterranean coastline, Turkey, and Cyprus. Introduced into South Africa, Australia, New Zealand and Chile.

Comments   *Lactarius deliciosus*, the saffron or delicious milkcap, or red pine mushroom, is a species of milkcap mushroom native to Southern Europe, Cyprus and the Anatolian peninsula. It is an ectomycorrhizal symbiote of *Pinus* pine trees, and has been introduced into the Southern Hemisphere via pine tree plantations (the Monterrey pine, *P. radiata*, is a favorite host in these cases).

L. deliciosus is a pleasant-smelling, large, squat, carrot-orange to carrot-red mushroom that has a convex to vase-shaped cap that is 4 to 14 centimeters in diameter, on a stout, often hollow stipe that is 3 to 8 centimeters tall. When cut, the mushroom bleeds an orange-red exudate. The fruiting bodies appear underneath their pine tree hosts from Late Summer to Mid-Fall.

While the saffron milkcap has been used extensively in Mediterranean cuisines for thousands of years, several other milkcaps are held in higher esteem, as it has a mild, or occasionally bitter flavor that is considered inferior to, for example, the bleeding milkcaps, *L. sanguifluus* and *L. rubrilacteus*. Allegedly, when Carolus Linnaeus first named the saffron milkcap as *"Galorrheus deliciosus,"* he assumed it tasted delicious due to smelling its lovely odor, without actually tasting it, and it is often assumed he confused it with other, better-tasting mushrooms, such as *L. sanguifluus.* Having said that, take care to not confuse *L. deliciosus* with other orange milkcaps that are not safe to eat, such as the Olympian milkcap, *L. olympianus*, of the Olympian Peninsula, Washington State, which is also orange, but has a white exudate and a bitter taste.

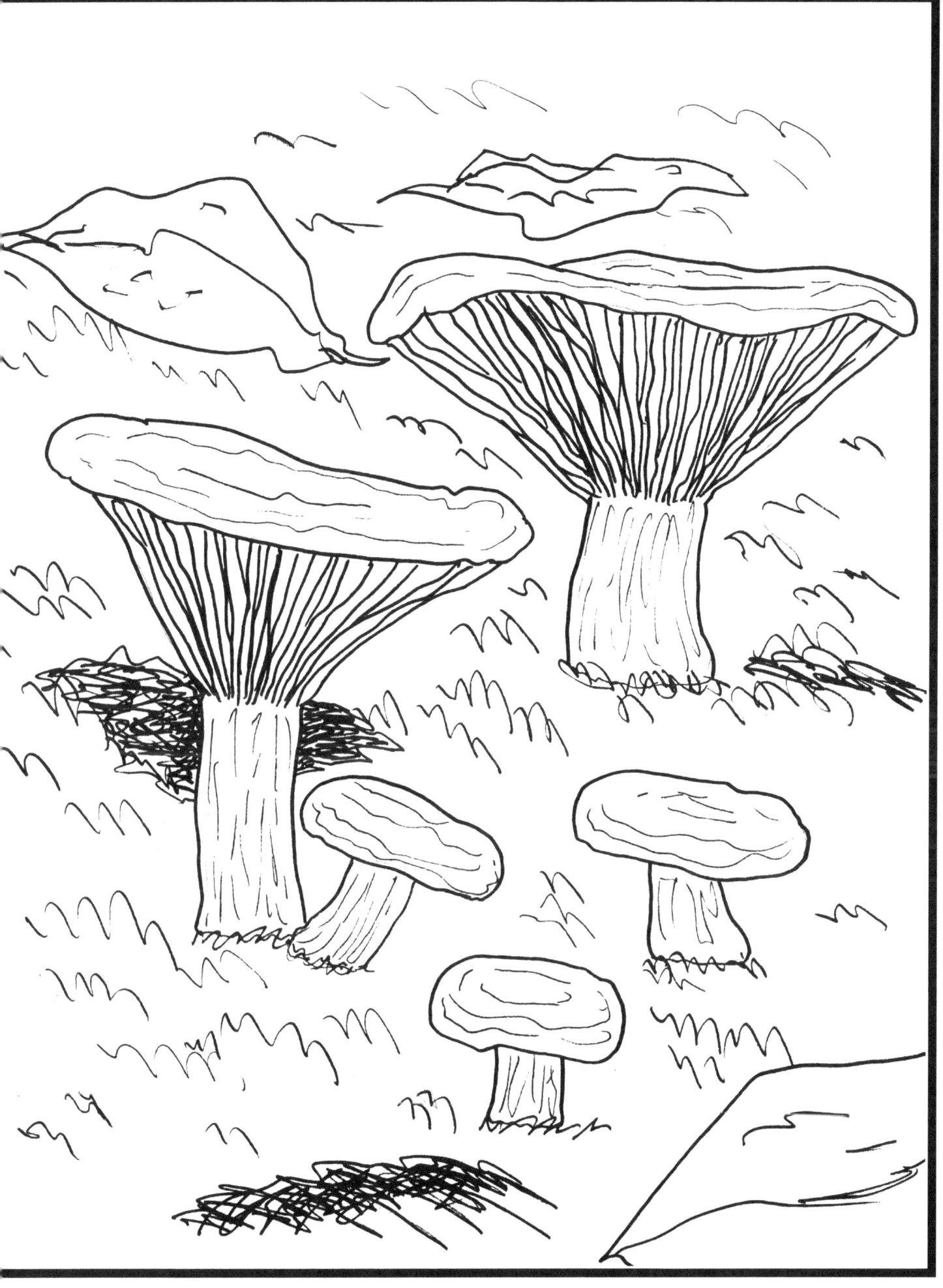

Name *Lanmaoa asiatica*

Location Subtropical forests of Yunnan Province, usually either pine forests or pine and oak forests.

Comments *Lanmaoa asiatica*, the Jiangshouqing, 见手青, is a species of choice edible bolete native to Southwestern China, where it lives as an ectomycorrhizal symbiote of the Yunnan Pine, *Pinus yunnanensis*, in Chinese subtropical forests. The common name translates as "see hand (turn) green/azure," and references to how touching the yellow pore surface or otherwise cutting or bruising it will cause the injured tissue to oxide a brilliant blue color.

The young fruiting body is initially a dark brown, but fades to a bright to pinkish red as the mushroom grows older. The porous underside of the 5 to 11 centimeter wide cap is an eggy spongecake yellow. The stipe is 8 to 11 centimeters tall. Fruiting bodies appear during the summer.

The generic name honors the Ming Dynasty scholar, Lan Mao (蘭茂), who, in his work, 滇南本草, ("Southwest Yunnan Materia Medica"), first coined the term "牛肝菌" (niúgānjùn), "beef liver fungus," which is now used to to refer to the cep, or edible bolete, *Boletus edulis*, in Chinese.

As mentioned, the jiangshouqing is a choice edible mushroom, comparable to the cep in terms of eating. However, eating the jiangshouqing raw leads to a situation the locals refer to as "看到小人人" (kàn dào xiǎo rénrén), or "seeing little people," where the mushroom eater sees fairies scurrying about due to ingesting hallucinogenic compounds that would otherwise break down during cooking. (As such, don't go to Yunnan for the specific purpose of going on a bolete bender, as consuming hallucinogenic substances in China is frowned upon by the local government)

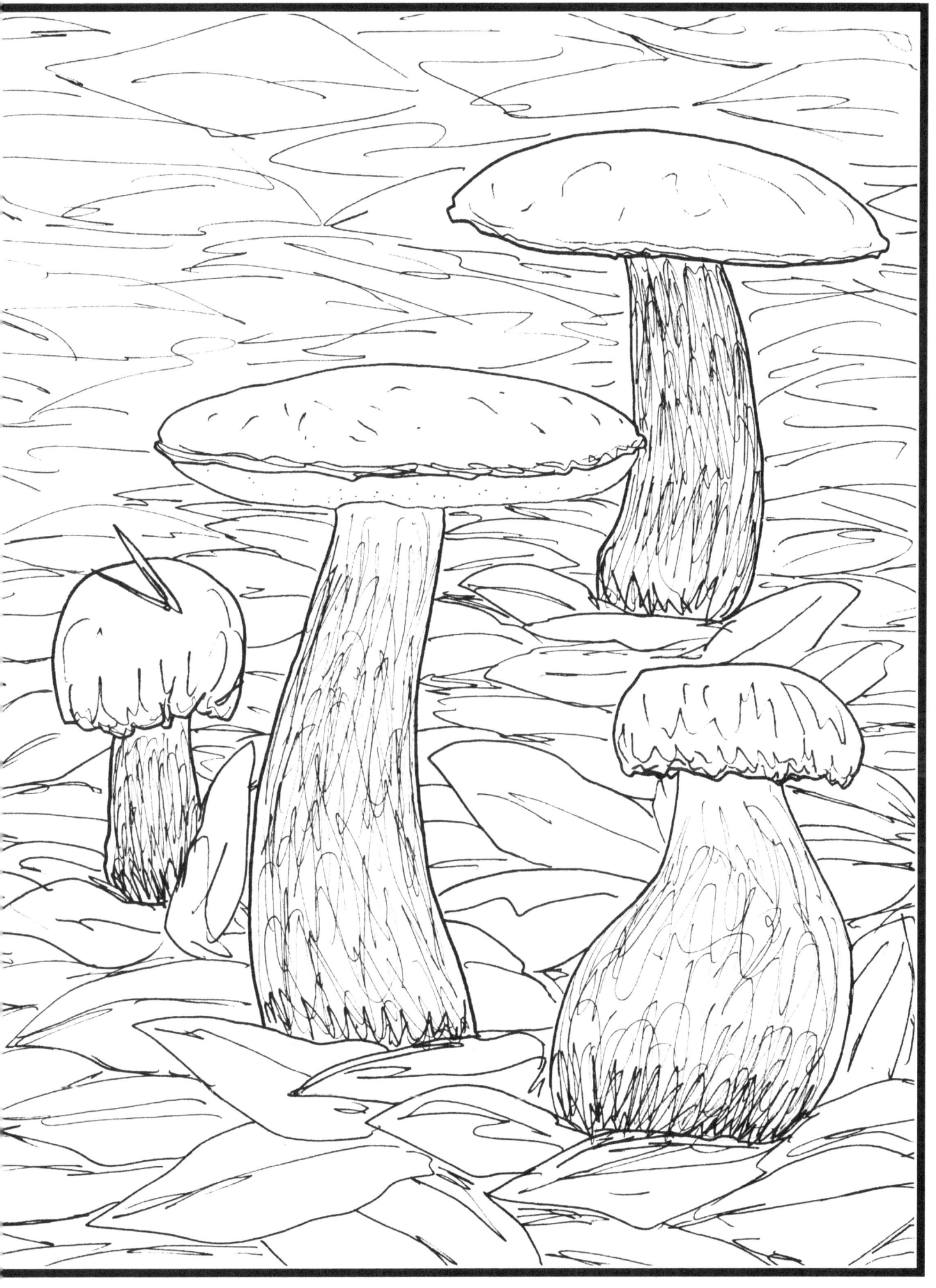

Name *Leotis viscosa*

Location Native to North American conifer forests.

Comments The Green Jelly Baby, or "Chicken Lips," *Leotis viscosa*, is a species of jelly baby fungus found primarily in mossier parts of North American conifer forests. Some authorities consider it a green-capped variant of the jelly baby, *Leotis lubrica*, but recent genomic analyses suggest that the two are not only separate species, but separate species complexes each consisting of numerous cryptic species (a group of genetically distinct populations composed of anatomically identical-looking individuals). All jelly babies are saprophytes, though, some evidence suggests they may form symbiotic relationships with blueberries and other North American species of *Vaccinium*.

When fresh or moist, the fruiting body is gelatinous, like a squishy gummy candy. The olive to bright to dark blue-green cap is 1 to 4 centimeters in diameter, sitting on a 2 to 8 centimeter tall, pale yellow stipe. The fruiting bodies appear from Early Spring to Autumn, or Early Winter in warmer climates.

Despite the fun common names, species of jelly baby are considered inedible due to their tastelessness and gelatinous texture making for a joyless eating experience.

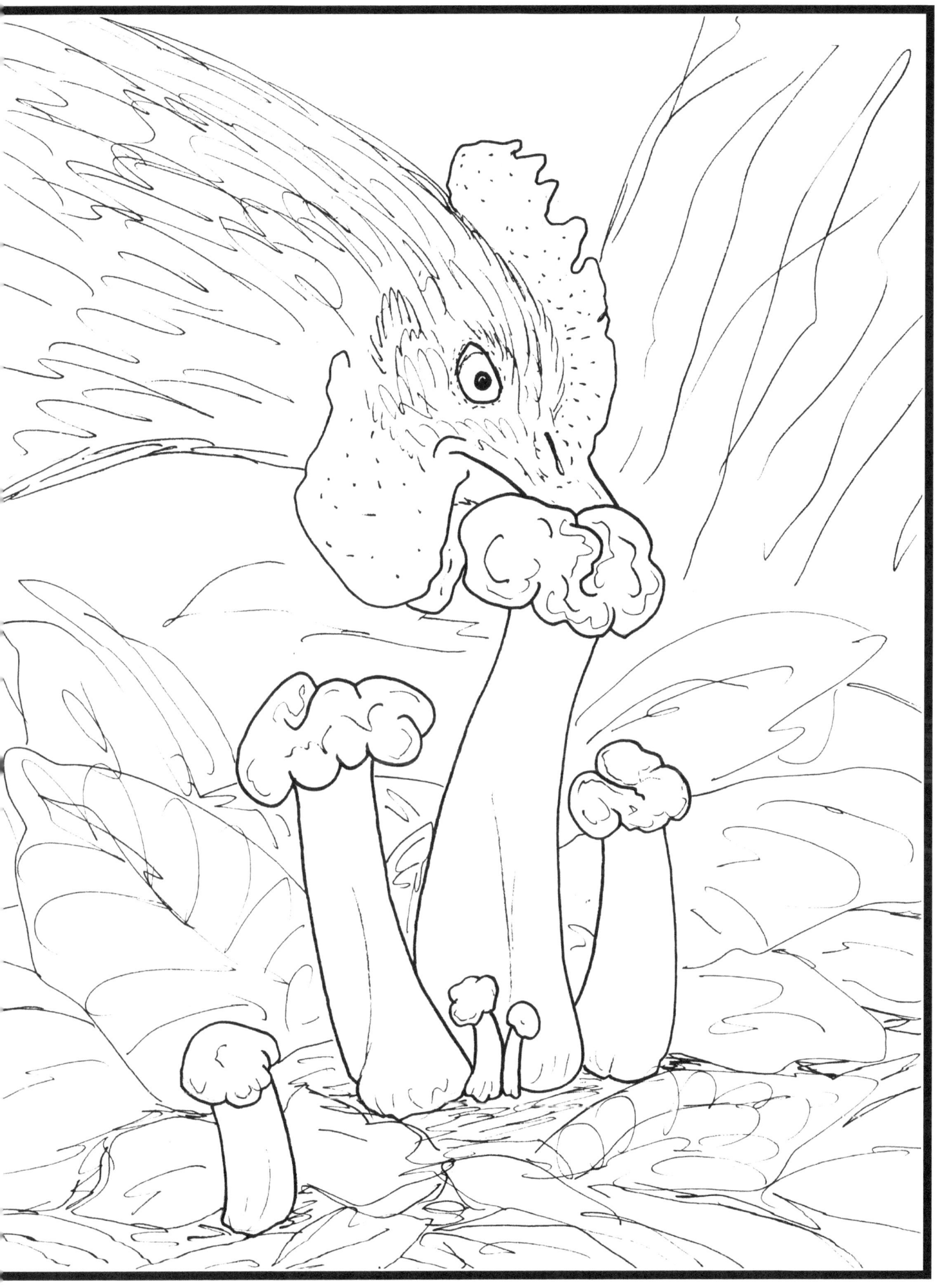

Name *Marasmius hudsonii*

Location Native to North America and Europe wherever there are holly (genus *Illex*).

Comments The Holly Parachute, *Marasmius hudsonii,* is a tiny species of parachute or pinwheel mushroom found in Europe and North America. As the common name suggests, *M. hudsonii* grows in association with holly bushes because it is a saprophyte that specifically feeds on rotting holly leaves.

The tiny, hairy caps are 1 to 5 millimeters in diameter, sitting on 10 to 20 millimeter long stipes, and are pinkish to off white in color, depending on age and humidity.

The specific name honors 18th Century English naturalist, William Hudson.

The holly parachute is considered a very rare mushroom partly because very tiny, super specific-niche mushrooms are difficult to find on principle, in general, and partly because *Marasmius*-specialist mycologists and mushroom writers specifically writing about the holly parachute are the only people who bother looking for this mushroom to begin with. By human standards, the holly parachute is inedible.

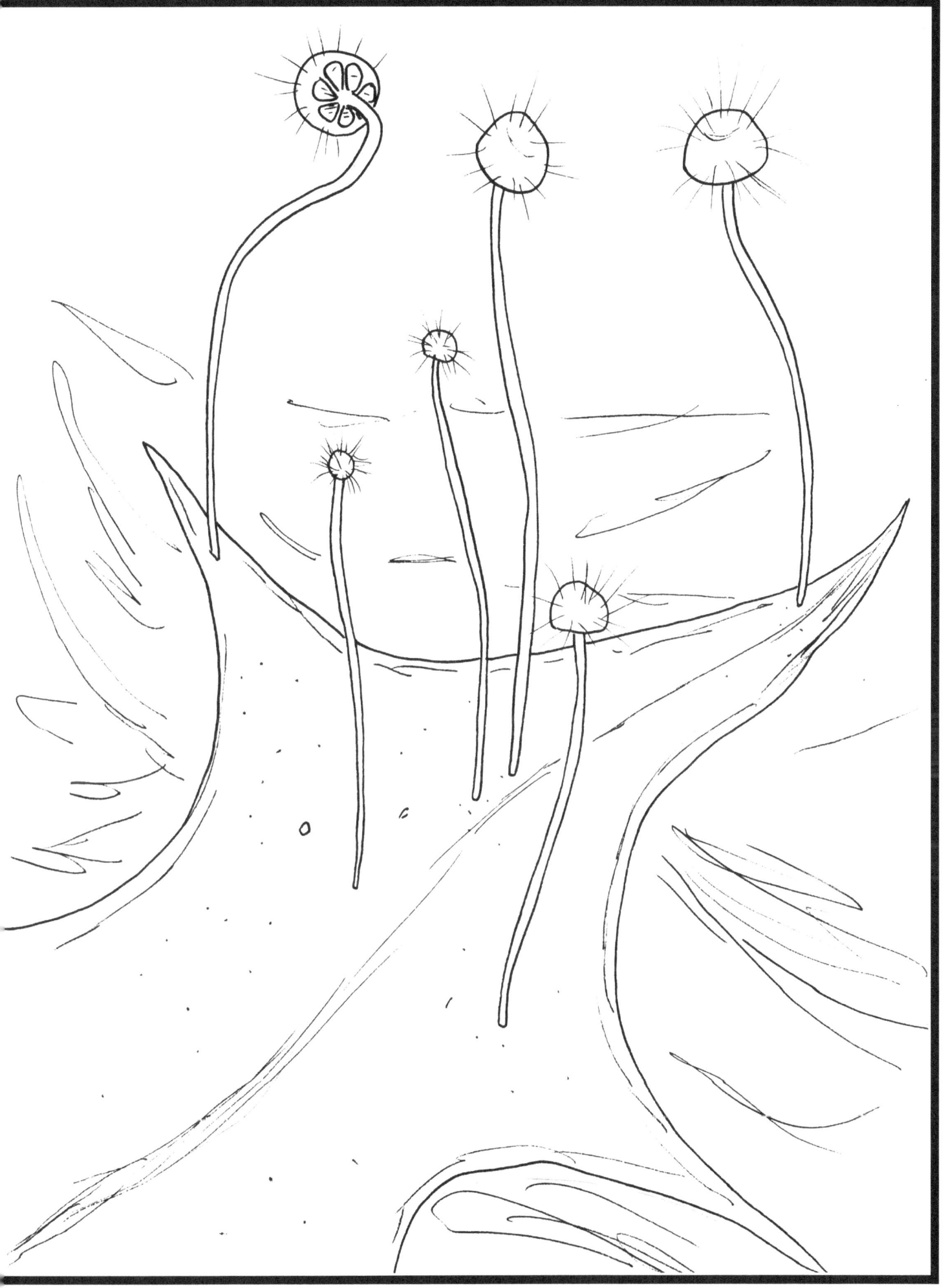

Name *Morchella esculenta*

Location Forests of Eurasia, North America, and possibly South America.

Comments The Common Morel, *Morchella esculenta*, is the best known species of morel mushroom. This large mushroom is found in forests throughout Eurasia and the Indian subcontinent, North America, primarily eastern and midwestern woodlands, and various parts of Brazil. Genomic tests suggest the common morel is conclusively native to Europe, and sightings elsewhere are either of doppelganger species, or introductions.

The distinctive, sausage gravy beige to dark brown cap is pitted, giving it a honeycombed or spongy appearance. The mature cap can be anywhere from 3 to 7 centimeters tall. The pale yellow stipe is 2 to 9 centimeters tall. The fruiting body is hollow, and often becomes infested with vermin; morel hunters often cut their quarry in half to better evict them of bugs and dirt. Common morels generally appear between Late Winter until Early Summer, often in conjunction with forest fires, as a spike in soil potassium will trigger a large bloom. Sightings of common morels appearing from the roots of elm trees dying of Dutch elm disease suggest that they are also opportunistic pathogens that will attack weakened host trees.

Common morels are facultative symbiotes that can live as saprophytes, but also thrive as ectomycorrhizal symbiotes of numerous deciduous tree species. Sightings of

While all morels are edible, and the better known species being prized edibles (with the common being chief among them), fresh morels can not be safely eaten raw due to the toxin hydrazine, which causes gastritis. Cooking fresh morels in wine or alcohol causes a chemical reaction that enhances the gastrointestinal irritating properties.

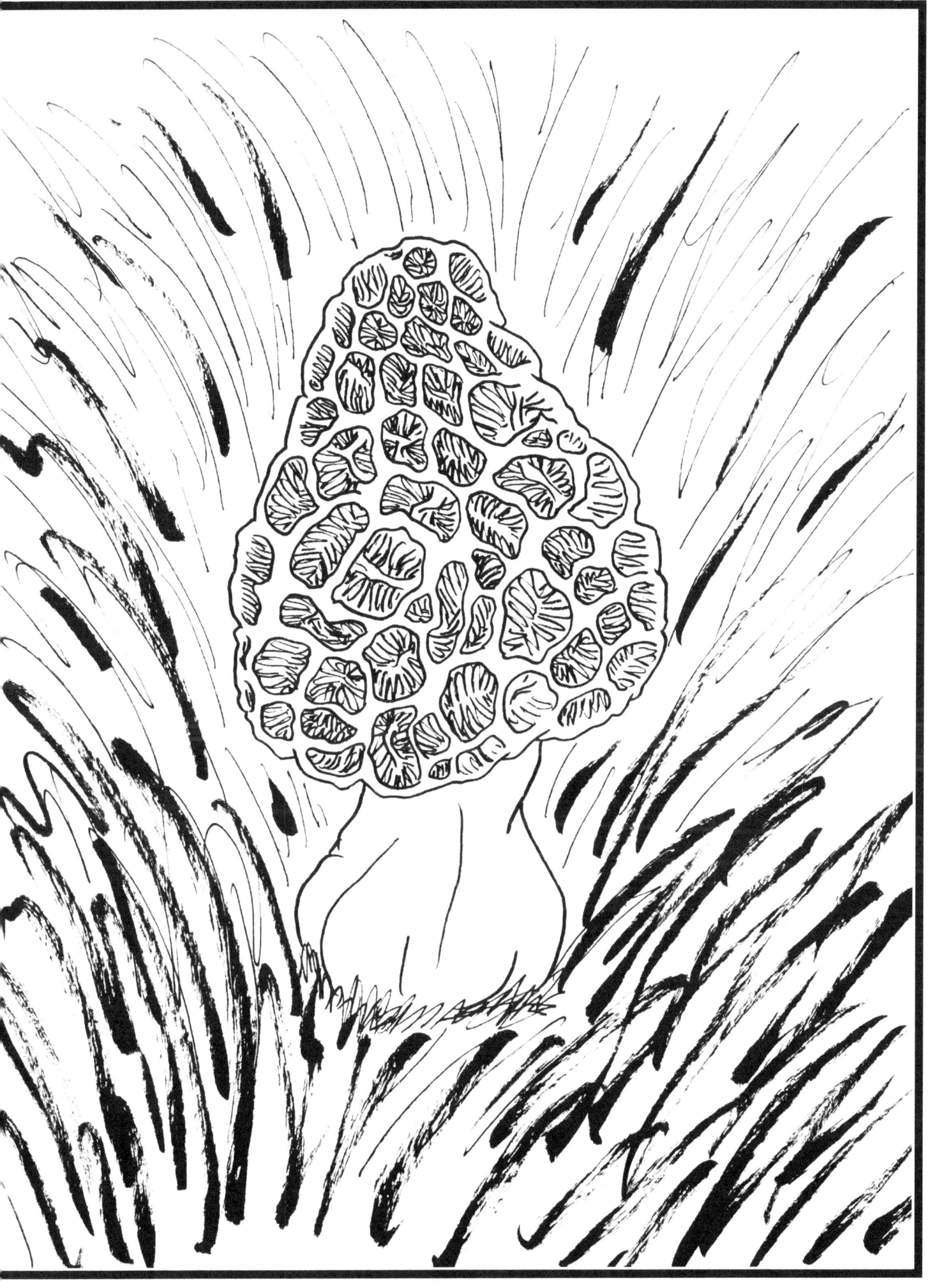

Name *Mycena epipterygia*

Location Forests and bogs of Europe.

Comments The Yellowleg Bonnet or Yellow-Stemmed Mycena, *Mycena epipterygia*, is a butter yellow bonnet mushroom found in diverse, but moist habitats across Europe, among forest moss, and especially in bogs. Unusually for bonnet mushrooms, the yellow-stemmed is edible. The fruiting bodies appear from Summer until Late Fall.

The fruiting body is small. The bell-shaped cap is faintly striated, possessed of a sticky cuticle, and is 1 to 2 centimeters wide. The cap may be pale yellow to a grayish brown, depending on humidity and its age. The stipe is very thin, no more than 2 millimeters wide, and is 2 to 9 centimeters long.

As mentioned, *M. epipterygia* is edible. However, due to its small size and the ease of confusing it with numerous other, similar-looking but poisonous mushrooms, mushroom experts recommend against eating them. In particular, the yellow-stemmed bonnet may be confused with the yellowing bonnet, *M. luteovariegata*, a poisonous relative with a fruiting body that is initially grayish lilac and turns a pale yellow as it ages. The yellowing bonnet is generally larger, found in fens (alkalinic wetlands), and often smells of radish like the lilac bonnet, *M. pura*.

Populations seen in the Pacific Northwest of North America are now referred to the species *M. nivicola*.

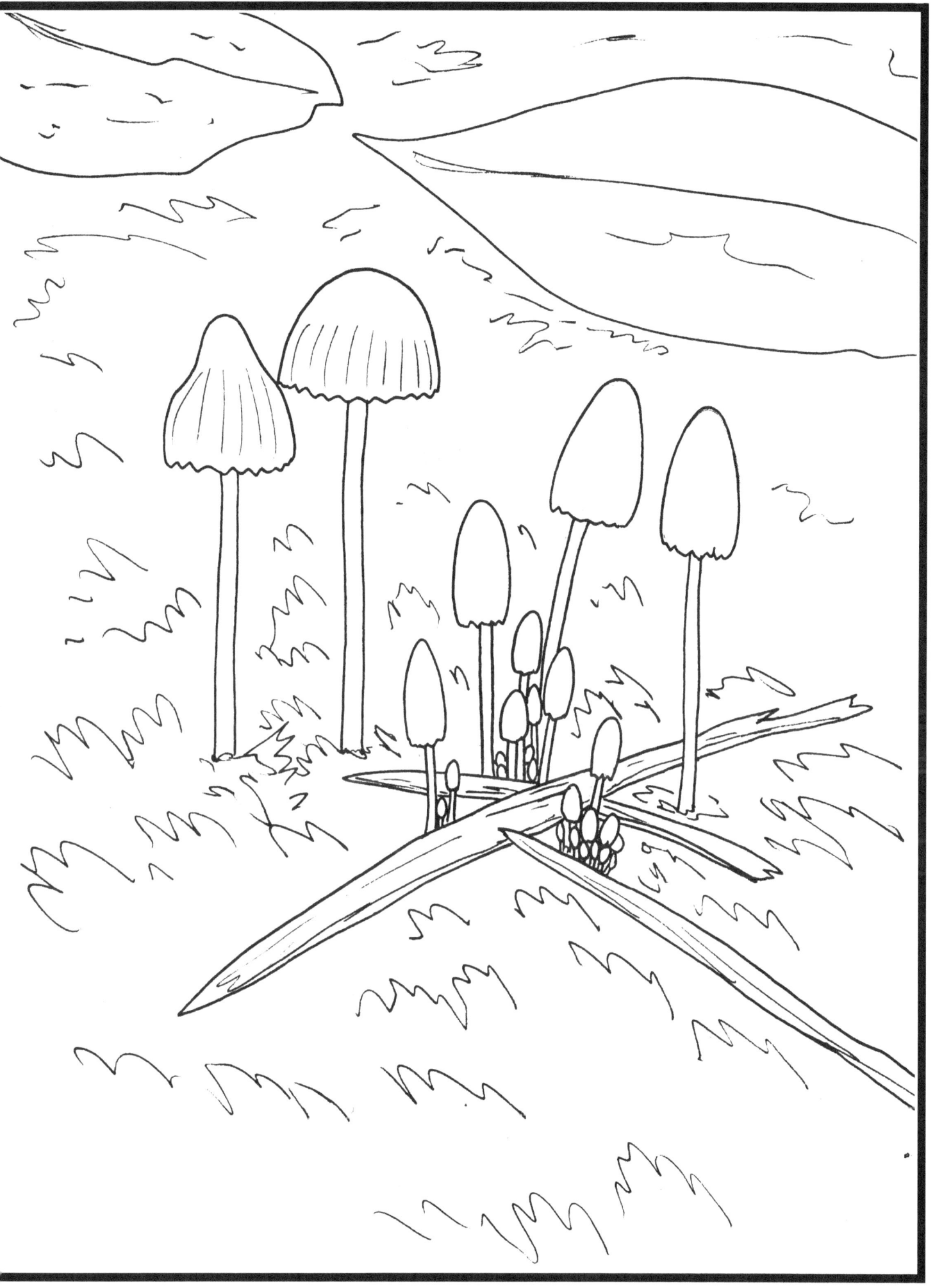

Name *Mycena pura*

Location Woodlands of Eurasia, Austronesia, and the Americas.

Comments The Lilac Bonnet, *Mycena pura*, is a species of bonnet mushroom found in forests throughout the world, except in Africa. The lilac bonnet is a saprophyte often associated with moss and rotting wood, and smells of radish. Despite its mild, pleasant taste, the lilac bonnet contains small amounts of the toxin muscarin, which can cause intense gastrointestinal distress if consumed.

As its name implies, the cap is usually a pale purple, though, depending on age, humidity, genetics, or whatever, the mushroom's coloration ranges from faded gray to a peachy flesh tone (those individuals on the latter end of the spectrum are often confused with the rosy bonnet, *M. rosea*, an equally poisonous relative that is larger and more robust, yet more adorable in appearance). White or yellow forms may be confused with the yellowing bonnet, *M. luteovariegata*, a denizen of fens (wetlands made alkaline due to limestone outcroppings) that is initially gray or lavender and turns yellow as it ages. The lilac bonnet is often confused with other small purple mushrooms, like various species of *Laccaria*, or the violet webcap, *Cortinarius violaceus*.

The cap is 2 to 5 centimeters wide on a thin stip no more than 8 millimeters thick and 4 to 8 centimeters tall. In temperate reaches of its range, the lilac bonnet appears from Summer until Mid Fall.

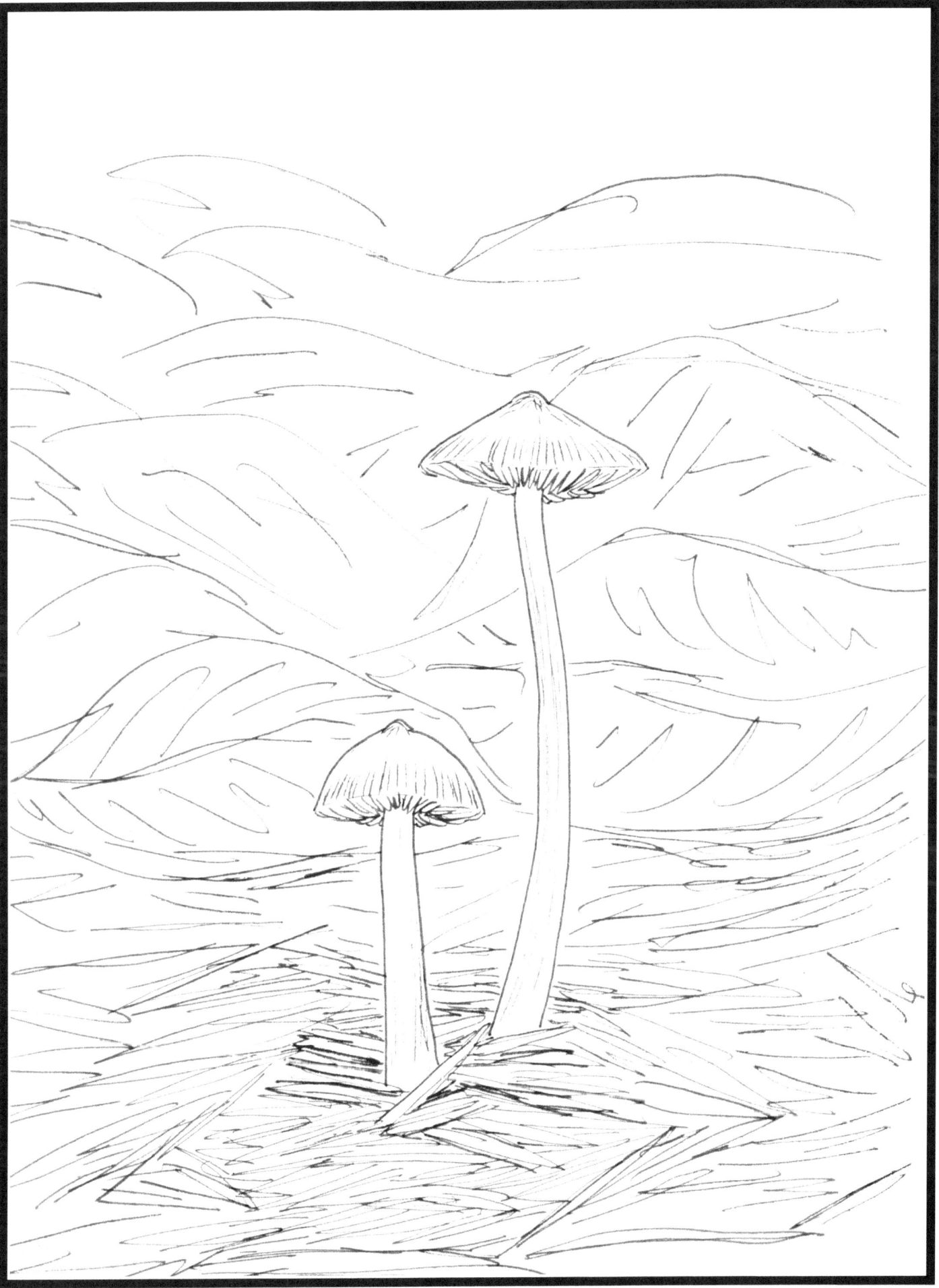

Name *Podoserpula miranda*

Location Southern half of Grande Terre Island, New Caledonia.

Comments The Barbie Pagoda, *Podoserpula miranda*, is an endangered species of ectomycorrhizal fungus known from five sites in the rainforests of southern Grande Terre Island (the main island) of New Caledonia. It is named "Barbie," as the fruiting bodies' coloration brings to mind the pink plastic accessories of a Barbie playset.

The bright pink to cotton candy pink fruiting bodies are up to 10 centimeters tall, and, unusually for mushrooms, but typical for species of *Podoserpula*, are stacks of three to six pilei. The Barbie pagoda is an ectomycorrhizal symbiote of the oak gum tree, *Arillastrum* gummiferum, and only grows in the soil of five of its host tree's stands.

Because the rainforests of New Caledonia are under constant threat of clearcutting, because the oak gum is specifically cut down for its economically valuable lumber, and because this fungus is rarely seen, the Barbie pagoda has been designated as a critically endangered species. Its edibility is unknown, though, other species of *Podoserpula* are considered too tough to be edible by human standards.

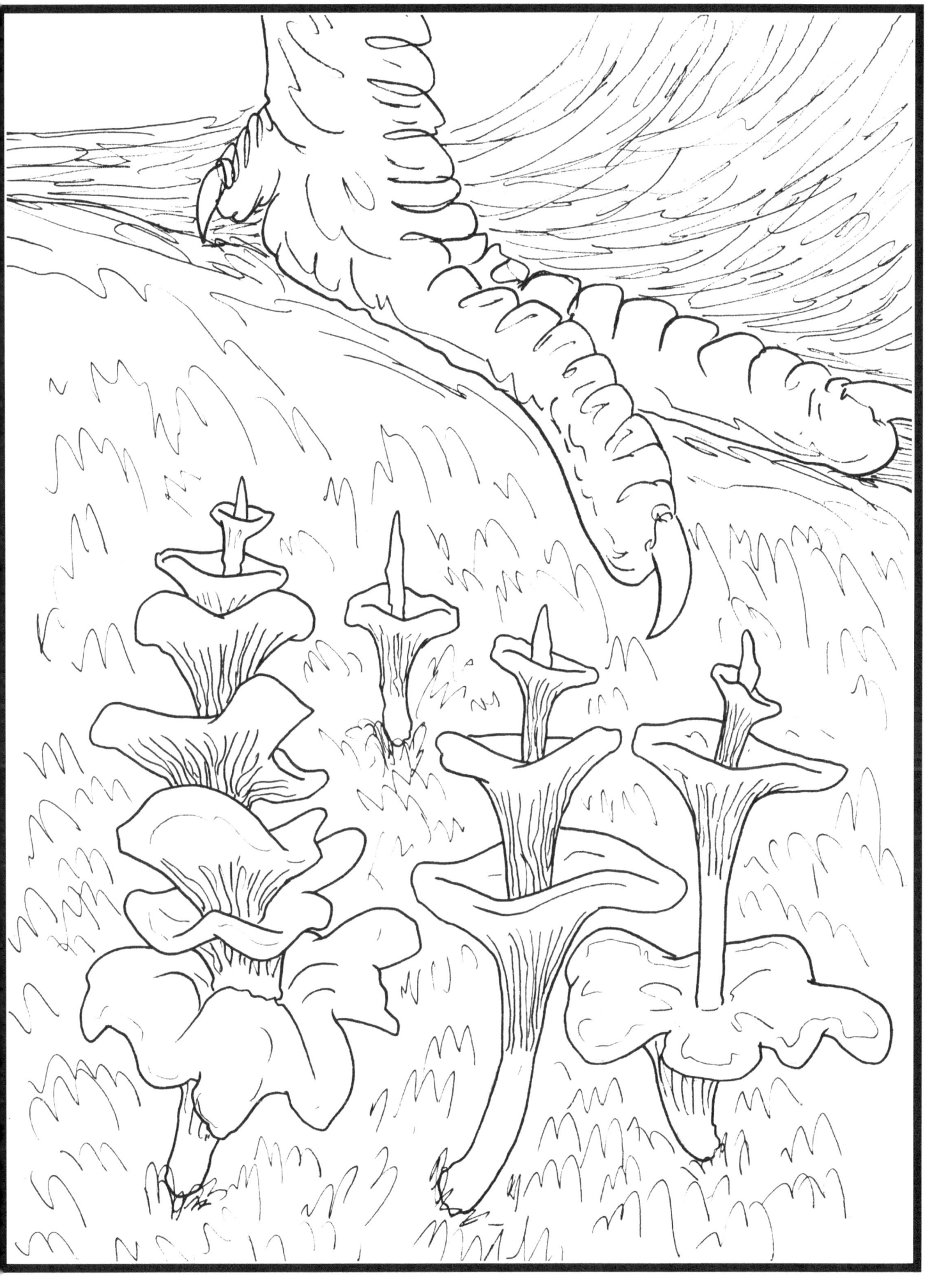

Name *Russula xerampelina*

Location Forests of the Northern Hemisphere.

Comments The Crab Brittlegill, *Russula xerampelina*, also known as the shrimp mushroom and shellfish-scented russula, is a large choice edible species of wide-ranging brittlegill found in forests throughout the Northern Hemisphere, from arctic and temperate coniferous forests, into tropical forests of Southeast Asia and Costa Rica. The crab brittlegill, named for its distinctive odor, is an ectomycorrhizal symbiote that prefers conifer trees as its hosts, (especially species of *Pseudotsuga* in the North American reaches of its range), but will also utilize larches and fagacid trees, as well.

The usually sticky cap is 6 to 20 centimeters in diameter, and is usually dark red or burgundy color (this is reflected in the specific name, which means "dry grape leaf."), leading to potential confusion with the sickener, *R. emetica*. Some strains are dark green, potentially leading to confusion with the green quilted russula, *R. virescens*, and the green russula, *R. aeruginea*. The stem of the crab brittlegill is 4 to 12 centimeters tall. In the more northerly parts of its range, *R. xerampelina* appears during Autumn.

The crab brittlegill is one of the most beloved edible species of brittlegill due to its large size, mild flavor, and the strong odor of cooked crab that allows for almost instant confirmation of identification.

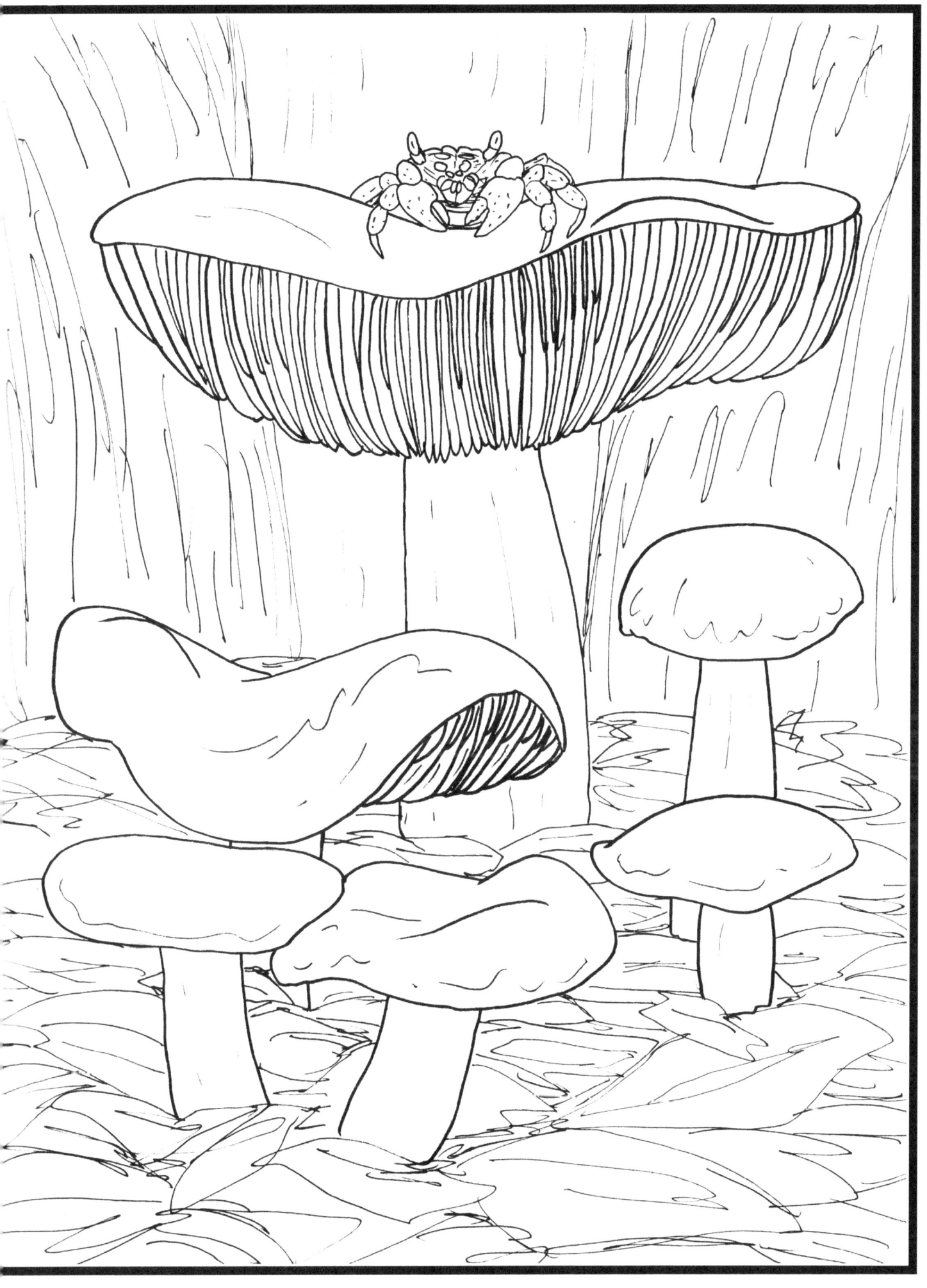

Name *Tricholoma equestre*

Location Mixed or coniferous forests of Eurasia and North America.

Comments The Man On Horseback, or Yellow Knight Tricholoma, *Tricholoma equestre*, is a large, toxic, yet prized edible mushroom found in forests of Eurasia and North America, where it lives as an ectomycorrhizal symbiote of *Pinus* pine trees in nutrient-poor, sandy soils.

The yellow knight is a butter to bright yellow color that darkens to a brownish yellow with age. The cap is 5 to 10 centimeters wide; its occasional irregularity leads to another common name of "saddle-shaped tricholoma." The stem is 5 to 7 centimeters tall. The fruiting body has an odor and flavor of wheat flour.

The man on horseback has long been a favorite food of European knights and nobility. Recent studies in conjunction with the correlation of mysterious deaths show that eating the yellow knight in large quantities or for a long term is potentially dangerous, as the mushrooms appear to have compounds that cause liver and kidney inflammation, leading to nausea, numbness, stiffness and weakness of muscles, and eventual death.

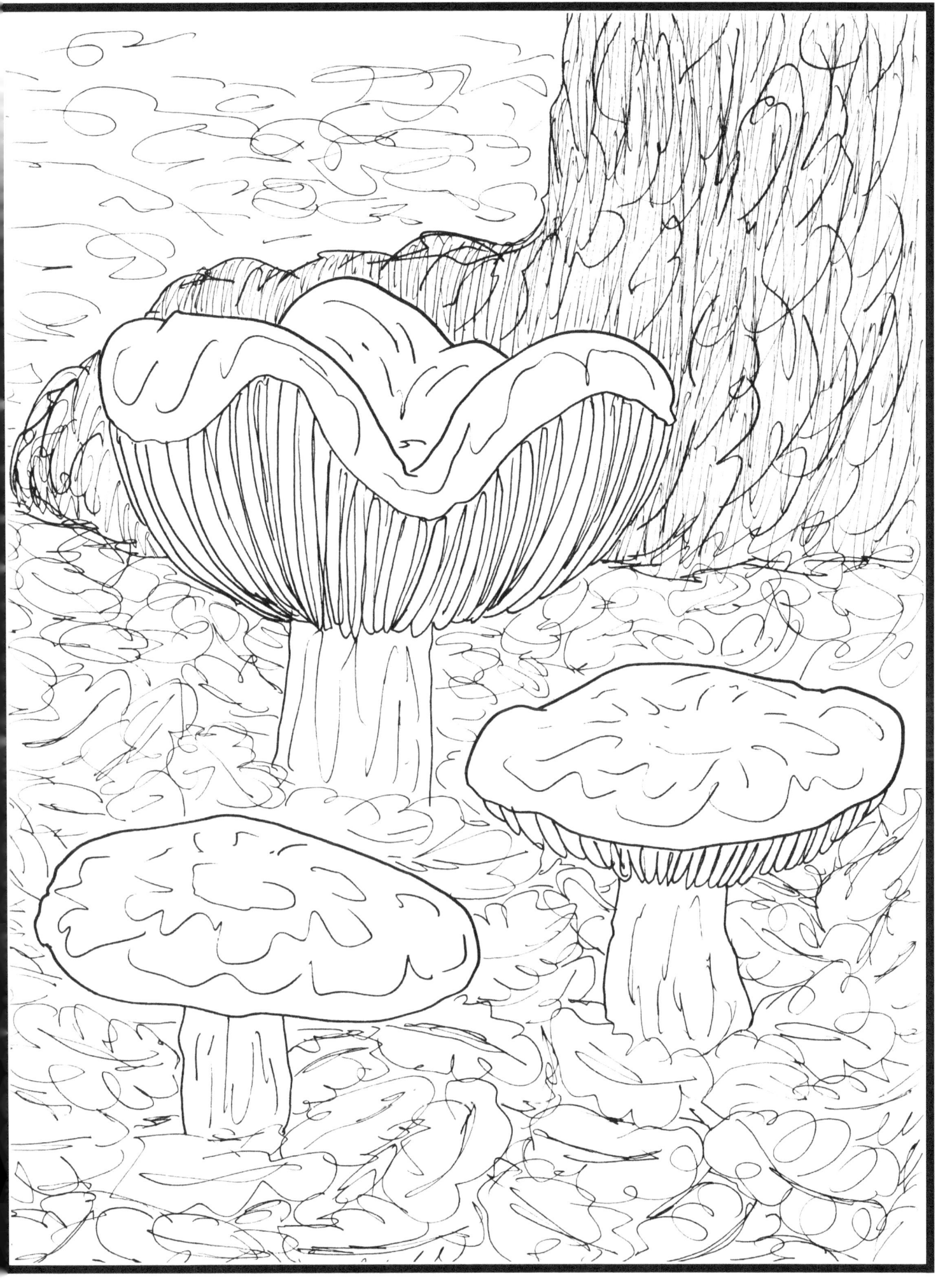

Bibliography

- Buyck, Bart, et al. "Podoserpula miranda sp. nov.(Amylocorticiales, Basidiomycota) from New Caledonia." *Cryptogamie, mycologie* 33.4 (2012): 453-461.
- Buyck, Bart, et al. "A multilocus phylogeny for worldwide Cantharellus (Cantharellales, Agaricomycetidae)." *Fungal Diversity* 64 (2014): 101-121.
- Cabral, Tiara Sousa, et al. "Abrachium, a new genus in the Clathraceae, and Itajahya reassessed." *Mycotaxon* 119.1 (2012): 419-429.
- Chai, Hui, et al. "New and noteworthy boletes from subtropical and tropical China." *MycoKeys* 46 (2019): 55.
- da Marcela Vasco-Palacios, Aí, et al. "Austroboletus amazonicus sp. nov. and Fistulinella campinaranae var. scrobiculata, two commonly occurring boletes from a forest dominated by Pseudomonotes tropenbosii (Dipterocarpaceae) in Colombian Amazonia." *Mycologia* 106.5 (2014): 1004-1014.
- De Kesel, André, et al. "New and interesting Cantharellus from tropical Africa." *Cryptogamie, Mycologie* 37.3 (2016): 283-327.
- Del Conte, Anna, and Thomas Laessoe. *The Edible Mushroom Book: A Gourmet's Guide to Foraging and Cooking*. Penguin, 2008.
- Dickinson, Colin, and John Lucas. "The encyclopedia of mushrooms." (1979).
- Gwladys, FADEYI Olyvia. "Diversity, conservation status and promotion of the genus Cantharellus in Benin (West Africa)." (2021).
- Hibbett, David S., David Grimaldi, and Michael J. Donoghue. "Fossil mushrooms from Miocene and Cretaceous ambers and the evolution of Homobasidiomycetes." *American Journal of Botany* 84.7 (1997): 981-991.
- Hobbs, Christopher. *Medicinal mushrooms: an exploration of tradition, healing, and culture*. Book Publishing Company, 2002.
- Hurst, Jacqui., and Lyn Rutherford. *A Gourmet's Guide to Mushrooms & Truffles* HPBooks, 1991
- Jordan, Peter, and Steven Wheeler. "The practical mushroom encyclopedia: identifying, picking and cooking with mushrooms." *(No Title)* (2003).
- Kim, Chang Sun, et al. "Two Newly Recorded Entoloma Species, E. eugenei and E. subaraneosum, in Korea." *The Korean Journal of Mycology* 43.2 (2015): 118-124.
- Lamaison, Jean-Louis, and Jean-Marie Polese. *The great encyclopedia of mushrooms*. Könemann, 2005.
- Lan, M. A. O. "Diannan bencao tushuo." *ZBQ*.
- Miller, Orson K., and Hope H. Miller. *North American Mushrooms: A Field Guide to Edible and Inedible Fun*. Falcon Guide, Globe Pequot Press, 2006.
- Saengha, Worachot, et al. "Exploring the Bioactive Potential of Calostoma insigne, an Endangered Culinary Puffball Mushroom, from Northeastern Thailand." *Foods* 13.1 (2023): 113.
- Trudell, Steve, and Joe Ammirati. *Mushrooms of the Pacific Northwest*. Timber Press, 2009.
- Vasco-Palacios, A. M., et al. "Austroboletus amazonicus (amended version of 2020 assessment)." *The IUCN Red List of Threatened Species* (2020): 2020-3.
- Winkler, Daniel. *Fruits of the Forest: A Field Guide to Pacific Northwest Edible Mushrooms*. Mountaineers Books, 2022.
- Ying, Chien-che. *Icons of medicinal fungi from China*. Science press, 1987.
- Zhu, Xue-Tai, et al. "The genus Imleria (Boletaceae) in East Asia." *Phytotaxa* 191.1 (2014): 81-98.

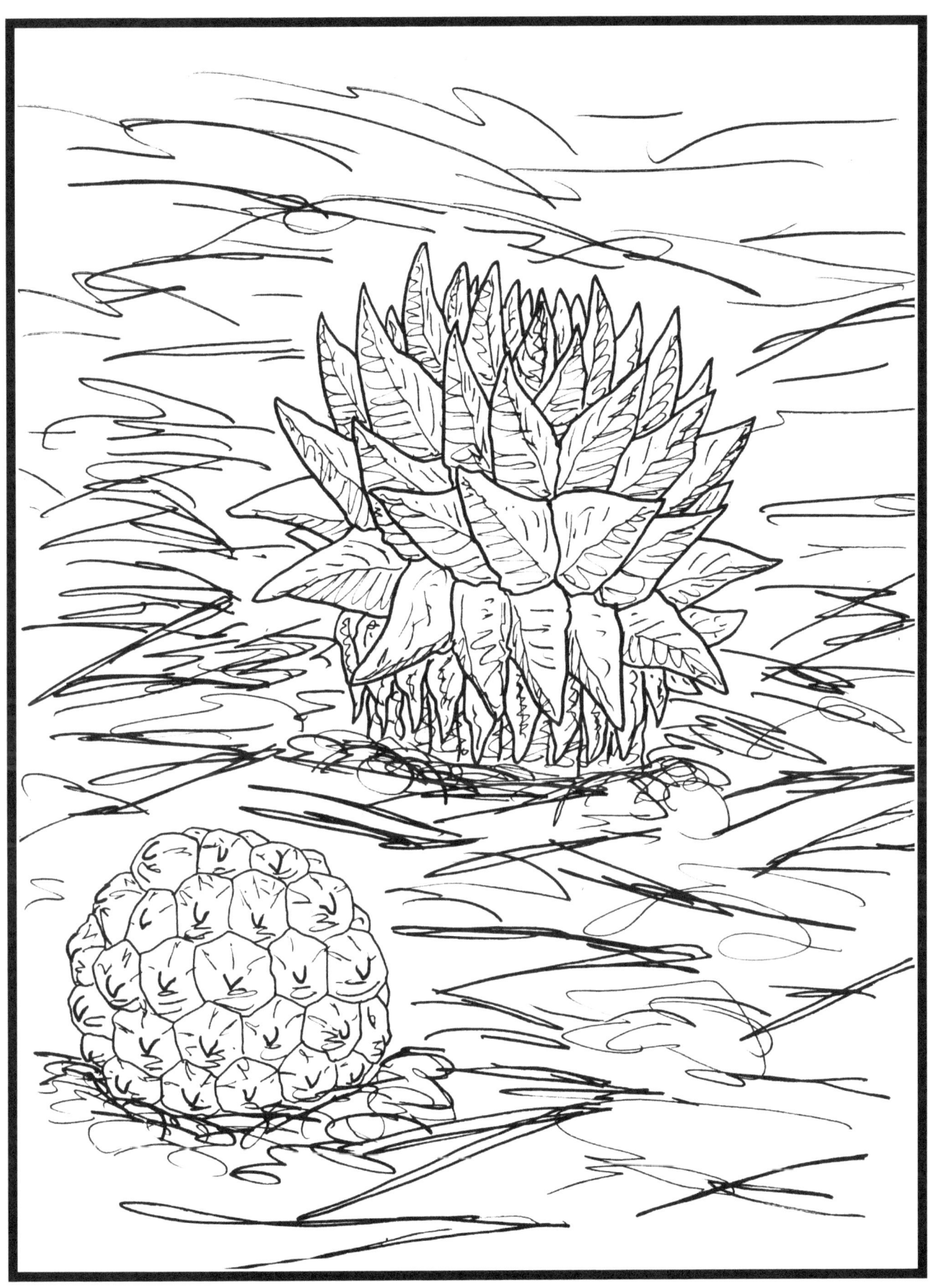

About the Artist

Stanton F. Fink is a student of Biology and Chinese Medicine, and makes a hobby of drawing monsters and researching flowers, arcane-looking creatures, prehistoric animals, fish, reptiles, birds and the occasional, really grotesque fungal fruiting body.

Stanton grew up and went to school in California and is currently living, drawing, and gardening in Oregon.

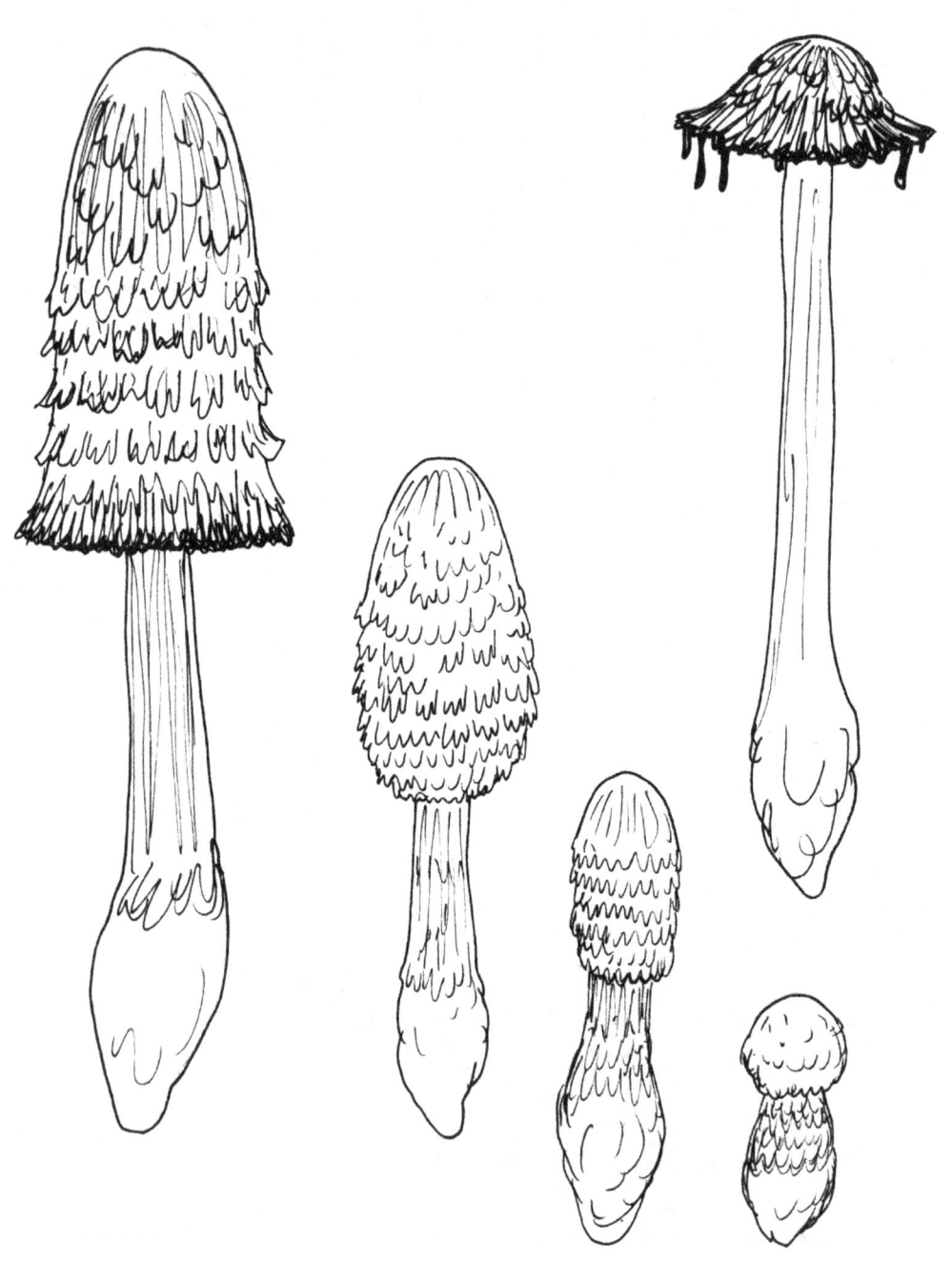

www.ingramcontent.com/pod-product-compliance
Lightning Source LLC
Chambersburg PA
CBHW081549240526
45470CB00024B/2929